Secondary Character
and Other Stories from
The Welsh Short Story Network

Edited by
Barrie Llewelyn

OPENING CHAPTER

First Printing, 2015

ISBN 10: 1-904958-58-3

ISBN 13: 978-1-904958-58-1

published by

Opening Chapter
Cardiff, Wales

www.openingchapter.com

To all the writers everywhere

Introduction
Barrie Llewelyn

I wasn't there at the beginning but I believe the formation of the Welsh Short Story Network occurred because several writers were discussing - how can I put this diplomatically? – the lack of focus on the short story in Wales. We have very few Welsh based publishers and even fewer magazines. Those that exist do a great service to the stories and writers they publish, but there simply aren't enough pages to accommodate the many, many writers who are writing good stories in Wales right now. The remit of the WSSN was to raise the profile of the form by gathering readers and writers together at events around the country. I was invited to take part in one of the Cardiff readings and on a summer's evening in the courtyard cafe at Chapter Arts Centre, the idea for this book was born.

Wait until you discover the diversity of the following stories, the variety of subject matter, the characters and narrative voices. I am proud that this collection illustrates that it's very hard to make rules about what constitutes a short story. Some stories take place in Wales, but many do not. All that the writers, represented here, have in common is that in some sense we identify ourselves as Welsh writers. Some are more published than others – but I bet you won't be able to know which ones – and I'm very proud of that too.

Thank you to all the writers who have given their stories and many thanks also to the publisher, Derec Jones at Opening Chapter and to Jo Mazelis for the cover design. This has truly been collaboration and all of us hope that this small thing, this book will lead to a greater thirst for and, maybe eventually, more opportunities for the short story in Wales.

This is, above all and as any anthology of short stories should be, a celebration of talent and imagination. So, please - enjoy!

Barrie Llewelyn
University of South Wales

STORIES

Колыма (Kolyma)
Rhys Thomas

The road stretches backwards and curls around a bluff. There is no road before us, just the great void of tundra. The Devil stands against the truck and he's smoking a cigarette, the perpetual grin on his face. I watch from the corner of my eye because if he sees me looking he'll put a bullet in me.

I've come to the realisation that I'll never see my family again and I've accepted it. It's funny how the cold will tame the soul. And hunger? That's even worse. Vaskov used to say he was the furnace-man of the soul. He knew how to grow cabbage and out in this tundra growing anything you can eat is alchemy. Back in the mines they kept him alive and fed him well because of his talent. And in return he gave us hot cabbage soup and this, he said, preserves our souls for the future. He seems like someone I knew in another life. The will to escape remains but it's faded so much that it hardly feels real any more.

The Devil throws down his cigarette in the same indifferent way I've seen him stand on the roof of a truck and shoot down into the top of a man's skull. He shoulders his machine-gun and pulls his collars around his scarf, blossoms of snow spinning around him.

'Come on, you pigs. Dig, dig, dig. I want to go home tonight. What do you think this is? A holiday?'

Building this road is worse than mining. At least when I was mining I knew I'd get to sleep in a bed at the camp. And it's always nice to find a piece of gold. One day I'll go back to that mine and I'll find my secret hiding place and recover my treasure and become rich.

I got transferred to the road one day at the start of winter. I don't know why but I know it must have had something to do with Chichvarkin. "Tax" he said, of the bread he forced me to give up. Tax? How can that man call himself a Communist? 'I know what you're up to, Yevgeny,' he'd say, of my secret gold. 'There's a tax on secrets.' Maybe he did know, maybe he didn't. Maybe he said this to everybody. I couldn't ask my friends because in the camps you never really know who's on whose side. So I started eating faster, hoping I'd be done before Chichvarkin could get to me. And now I'm here, somewhere on the way to Magadan, carving this road.

I push my shovel into the earth and press my feet down and the metal clunks into the icy soil. I stand on the shovel but I've lost so much weight it hardly makes a difference.

'Hey!'

The Devil has seen some fun. Iosif has fallen. Tiny crystals of snow waft across the world and dapple the mud. Iosif tries to stand but it's too hard for him, his body is a clatter-bone latticework on all fours. The zest of energy left him days ago. A brutal kick up into his guts nearly lifts him off the ground. He rolls over and splats into a slushy puddle and his gasping breath comes out as a cloud of steam.

'Get up you lazy shit or we'll put you in the road. How'd you like to spend eternity with the rumble of Papa Stalin's trucks chugging over your head?'

All Iosif can do is shake his head.

'What's that? I can't hear you?'

The small frame of the Moskvich clutches his fingers into winter trees as if they could stop a bullet. The Devil grins down the barrel of his machine-gun.

'Ha! Get up, you slug. I'm not going to shoot you.' Then he pushes the muzzle further into Iosif's face.

Everybody watches, nobody says anything.

'I'm just kidding with you,' the Devil laughs. He waves to the other guards. 'Pathetic, isn't it?'

The other guards smile but it's clear that even they can't stand him. He turns back to Iosif, flips the machine-gun round and slams him in the side of the head. I see the eyes roll back in his head as he falls onto his side. Iosif was a scientist before being collected by the shadows. I spoke to him once, a hushed, stilted discourse from which I learned he was a medical researcher, and for putting his faith in that church, he is now dead.

The Devil kicks him a few times, trying to rekindle the spark of life but it's never going to come back because the spark deserted Iosif weeks ago and what remained was a ticking mechanical shutdown.

We turn away and carry on digging.

The sun, invisible behind a mass of cloud, sinks and with it goes what little temperature there is. My hands seize, the moisture on the exposed parts of my face freezes, and it is all I can do to hold on to thoughts. I think of Leningrad and the Neva, of walking the banks of the river at midnight. My two boys and my wife – where are they now? The night I was taken flashes at the back of my mind; a bang in the dark, voices, lights swinging across walls, violence. And that was that, a wound cauterised without choice, an old life ending and a new one beginning, just like that.

It is just before dark that the Devil commands us to

dig a hole in the middle of the road. We work slowly and silently, just like always, and when it is done it takes five of us to carry Iosif's corpse across to the hole where we deposit it without emotion. We cover him up and there he is, a part of the road forever, just like The Devil said. I lay my shovel down and sit in the wet mud. The line of the horizon shines a moment and I see, there on the top of the hill, the outline of a great bear. It paws a few steps and stops and its head turns to us. Nobody else notices.

When I first got transferred I calculated intricate escape plans. We were out in the wilds with hardly any guards. Having gained the trust of a few other men we would talk and laugh about how we could get away. Laugh because there was of course no escape. Even if we could get away from the guards where in hell would we go? We joked that we'd freeze ourselves in a pool until summer and then thaw out and return home bedecked in glory. Those men I laughed with died a while back now but my dreams of escape live on, just, however ludicrous. You have to keep hoping.

The winter deepens and men fall in their hundreds and their bodies end up in the same place as Iosif. Is this road really worth this? For months I survive and know not why – everybody else who came here in the same truck as me is dead. We cut our way across Siberia at a snail's pace. The road isn't even surfaced with anything for the most part. Wide rivers, frozen in winter's breath, are traversed and no thought is given to the summer, when the rivers will melt and become impassable. Maybe some other sad gulag bastards are coming behind us to build bridges. We're told nothing.

The bear is following me. I see him from time to time. He always keeps a safe distance and I put this down to the fact he can smell The Devil. The snow is so thick in parts that it takes half the morning to clear before we can even reach the frozen soil. Still, this road will service an empire one day. We're cutting a new vein for Mother Russia.

We have arrived at a nomadic camp and the farmers have been obliged to give us food and drink. The Devil has discovered a secreted carafe of camel milk and is taking great pleasure in watching our reactions as we drink it but the joke is on him because I enjoy the taste. Whether by refinement or chance it tastes sweet and watery. It's been warmed over the fire and when it falls into my belly I feel it extend down through the root system of my body. Of course I grimace; The Devil expects nothing less.

'Old man.' He's talking to the tribal elder. 'Tell us a story. That's what you retards do to amuse yourselves isn't it? It's not as if you can pop along to the local whore house is it?' And he snorts his repulsive, forever lonely laugh.

The elder lifts his head to the vast array of stars. His Russian is poor but serviceable. He tells a story of a race of tall men who came to Earth in ancient times and the Devil seems sated.

The nomad sitting next to me nudges my ribs. 'Here,' he whispers, and he hands me some wet green matter and gestures to his mouth to say, eat it. I bring the matter to my lips. It tastes salty and its texture is moist.

At the end of the night The Devil ensures our installation in the nomads' yurts. The animal pelts soothe and warm me and I feel groggy. I close my eyes and fall asleep…

… and awake to the sound of the moon. She breathes so softly over the world the only thing that can feel her are the tides. I steal from the yurt and look about me. There is a guard over by the dying fire but I can tell I'm invisible to him. They don't worry too much about guarding us at night because if we run we'll be frozen by morning. Or maybe not. I glide silently by the guard and strike out across the surface of the frozen snowfield. I have escaped and Mother Russia will shield me from the cold because she is whispering promises to me as I go. I find a pine forest and navigate quickly and easily through. The forest guides me and I do not feel the cold. I clamber up a denuded rock face stubbled with brush and canter along the edge of an escarpment. The moonshine makes the tops of the pines look like one massive thing that bends and throbs with the heartbeat of the planet.

As the sun clears the curve of the earth and burns away the cloud into a deepness of indigo I feel sleepy and I lay down and am gone.

When I wake I remember my attempted escape. What the hell did that nomad give me? It doesn't matter – whatever it was its effects have worn off and I now realise it's going to do me in. I look down at my body and thank god I enshrined myself in one of the animal pelts from the yurt because apart from that I am wearing nothing. I'm going to lose my feet to frostbite and the rest of my body will follow not long after. I bet Chichvarkin would be laughing if he could see me now. Well at least he'll never find my gold. I pull the pelt tighter around me.

The cold pierces right down to the tiny networks of pain sensors, crystallising them into furry icicles. So this is how it all ends for old Yevgeny. There's no way I can get back to safety without decent clothes and boots. And even if I had clothes and boots the odds are still a million to one against. Still, these past few years, I've resigned myself to things far worse than death.

In the dark of my animal pelt I think of when things were better. In that other life I remember walking along the river to the hospital where I cured people, and taking long lunches with Vladilien, talking about politics and literature and our burgeoning love affairs, he with Svetlana, me with Valentina. I wonder what's become of him. I simply do not know. I think of Lev and Nik, my boys – are they still alive? There's no information and that lack of knowledge carves into my heart, digging out great scoops.

And Valentina. My last memory of her is a scream.

I don't know how much longer I can keep myself awake. My throat stings. I've been under this pelt for how long? Minutes? Hours? Days? If only I had some clothes. Then I might stand a chance. What I'd give for a comfortable pair of boots and a warm hat. Time slips and flickers and I hear a scratching sound nearby. Holding my breath I try to listen through the heavy wash of the cold. Something is looking at me and I know instinctively that it is the bear. I lift the pelt and sit up, turning my head in the direction of the sound. But it's not the bear.

'You thought you could get away?'

The Devil smiles. He leans against a tree and smokes his cigarette.

I'm so cold I can't answer.

'What's the matter? Don't you like making roads? How else can we get to Magadan if not by road, huh? Aren't you willing to put in a bit of effort for Mother Russia?'

'P-p-please,' I whisper.

'Look at you grovelling. What were you thinking?

You thought you could escape me? You think you can get away from someone like me in a place as open as Siberia? The road to Kolyma might be long, but it's not long enough for me to lose my sense of godliness.'

My teeth chatter madly in my mouth. My hands have lost feeling. I can sense my chest seizing. I want to freeze to death before he can shoot me. That at least will be something.

'The ability to track people has always stood me in good stead.' He taps the end of his cigarette. His smile never ends. 'The powerful spend a disproportionate amount of time simply looking for their enemies, and I cut that time away like baked flesh off a bone.' He stands upright from the tree. 'In return they allow me certain... cruelties, of which I know you have witnessed many.' He steps forward. I can see why people call him The Devil now. It's more than just a name, there is something *otherly* about him. 'I would have killed you in the end whatever. I know you used to be a doctor. You're not some dummy and you've seen way too much. I've been a very naughty boy out on this road and I can't have you telling tales, Yevgeny. Not if things go wrong. I must close every angle.'

My skull is being crushed by the cold. The Devil flicks his cigarette to the ground. The snow buzzes horizontal. The Devil exhales. Take me, cold. He raises his machine-gun. The snow thickens. There is a dark blur of motion from the trees, the ground shakes, the air roars, the Devil turns and is thrown sideways by some great force, his whole body lifted from the ground and propelled into the trunk of a pine tree.

He tries to stand, bringing his gun back round to me; he'd rather kill me than protect himself. The bear reaches him in two strides. Its jaws open and clamp

8

down on the guard's face and the bear shakes him, shakes him so hard I think his head might fall off. The face comes away with a sucking slurp. A wheel of red sprays into the air. The Devil turns to me with his flayed face, one eyeball still in its socket, the other dangling free, and he smiles.

The bear and I gaze at one another for a series of moments. Then, disinterested, he turns and disappears back into the forest.

Using the very last inches of my life spark I crawl over to the Devil. Everything will be okay. My hope rises in a fizzing rush. I use the warmth of his body to warm my own, the life returns to me, and then I take his clothes. I pull his fur hat over my head and feel the cogs of my mind turn faster. I pull on his warm shirts and gloves and coats and boots that will keep me warm my journey back to Leningrad. I could go back for my gold but that can wait. I need to find my family first. I take the Devil's pack and find food and water and vodka and those cigarettes of his. The brand is nameless – there is just a picture of a green lizard with a red stripe running up its back. Then I pick my way through the pine forest, totally ignorant of the way home. I have no idea where I am or the direction in which I am travelling. In truth, I am lost.

I cross a gravel delta. Water braids its way towards the sea. This is the first running water I've seen in months and this message, that spring is coming, kindles my spark. I cross the water and close my eyes. I run and fall to my knees. Joy drizzles through me as I open my eyes and stare down the long dark ribbon of road I have spent so long in building. The road-workers are all east of me, digging towards Magadan. And I'm heading west. And this road will show me the way home.

~

Rhys Thomas is the author of *The Suicide Club* and *On The Third Day*, published by Transworld Publishers. He lives in Cardiff and is slowly working on a third novel.

Of **Kolyma,** he says, 'My old cricketing team mate and fellow author, John Williams, asked me to write a story about a road for one of his *In Chapters* nights. I'd always been fascinated by the Road of Bones in Russia, which was built during the Stalinist era by gulag labour, and I also wanted to make sure the story had a completeness to it – I would be reading it aloud to a crowd so it was important to keep their attention.'

The Dyer's Apprentice
Nigel Jarrett

He shows her three sketches. One is a portrait of a young apprentice dyer, his apron and elbow-length gloves stained blue and orange. In the second, what looks like a huge carpet is pegged on a clothes line and hanging or drying indoors, its colour an intense blue with orange streaks. The third appears to have a piece of wallpaper pasted to it but it's really his drawing of a dull wallpaper pattern, with diagonal rows of a crescent moon in grey against a light beige background.

He says the portrait has been sketched with the help of two images: a magazine photograph of a young male model and an illustration of a dyer from olden times. He says the sketches are preparations for a bigger picture, in which the young dyer will be placed to the right, in front of the wallpaper, and the suspended carpet – actually a large piece of dyed hessian – will take up the left half. It was important that the wallpaper should be dull, 'beige-ish', and the dyer should be half-hidden, in the shadow of the thing he'd dyed.

She's told that the idea for the picture came to him from no source that could be specifically located. This was how artists worked, how art came about. There would be more sketches before work began on the painting and their completion would signal the extent of his search for its essential components.

She nods as he speaks, not looking at him; still not looking at him, she begins removing her clothes.

"Are you surprised I agreed to this?" she asks.

"You bet. Why did you agree to it? It's not as though you owe me a favour."

"Well, I was curious."

He starts to draw her with charcoal on a thick pad held before him between hand and upper arm, the arm bent at the elbow. "About what?"

"Oh, you know – us; you and me. After all this time."

They met by accident the week before at a preview of an exhibition at which his work was featured. She followed his career after a fashion. He isn't famous but he shows regularly. There are sometimes mentions in the 'what's on' lists. They talked. Something about each other seemed to imply revaluation and forgiveness. The guilt, once the province of the other, now seemed to be shared, or even disproportionately admitted. "You should sit for me," he said, half joking. "Name the day," she said. Since the break, they'd emailed each about three times.

She stops talking, just keeps staring in the direction he's indicated. She can hear him behind her, hear the swift marks he's making with the charcoal as well as those moments when the stick breaks and he has to blow away the dust and splinters. She can hear him rubbing the page, smudging the marks, blowing. A few of the floorboards squeak as he moves around. The studio extension to his flat, actually one of its original bedrooms, is cool and carpeted. She feels comfortable in all sorts of ways. It's a large expensive place. He was never a bohemian.

He gazes at her, his head cocked. He steps forward,

re-arranges her left arm, her head. Her shoulders are covered in goose bumps and her nipples are raised and pointing in different directions, like gun emplacements. He chuckles at that. She's never had a baby. He's employed models who've been mothers – are mothers. They're different visually and physically. They've done things, where she hasn't. She's not gone through the hurt of childbirth and motherhood as they have. He wonders if, once she's endured the hurt, she will think it worth repeating. One or two of the others have grown-up children – well, teenagers – yet their carnal desires trump what one might expect to be an instinct for guarded parental responsibility. Not that it often came to anything. When it did, they were both mature about it – or 'adult', as their sort used to say. The artist-model relationship was not always just a business arrangement, not now or in the past. His drawing of the naked female model was more than an anatomy lesson, though in employing models at an hourly rate his intention was to practise a skill that insisted on being exercised. He liked to think it would be the same for a woman artist hiring a male model, but the gender games had probably ruled that out as a simple reversal of roles. Into a dull old studio relationship he had tried to rub some significance.

"You're looking – really good," he says, immediately regretting the remark, one of those things that now have a dual meaning, though he intended it as a compliment. She *is* looking good. He wonders if in her eyes he is too. She appears not to take offence.

"Why shouldn't I be?"

"It's been fifteen years."

"Fifteen! Have you been counting?"

"It's a rough guess. About fifteen. Certainly fifteen."

"Actually, it's been thirteen years," she says. "Thirteen years, four months and twelve days."

Her head drops slightly and her eyes try to catch his but he isn't looking her way and she straightaway recovers her position. "You've changed."

"Really? I mean, of course I have. I must have. We all have. In all sorts of ways. Yes, I have changed. What's the obvious one would you say, the most noticeable difference?"

"You seem..."

She inadvertently moves her arm.

"No! Try not to..."

"Sorry."

"I seem what?"

"Well, actually, smaller. Diminished."

"Thanks!"

He knows exactly what she means but he says nothing. He cannot get the figurative meaning of 'diminished' out of his head. He doesn't think he's grown smaller. Perhaps a very slight stoop, the world on his shoulders and all that.

"Not to you, though," he says. "I can see."

"Well, I'm younger than you. Always have been."

She giggles. She feels warmer now. The conversation has distracted her from the apartment's middling temperature. Recomposing herself without altering her position too much, she recalls how painfully tedious modelling could be.

"Oh, yes. I forget. How could I have forgotten? What was it your old man said? 'He's a bit grown up for you, isn't he, old girl?' I was eavesdropping."

"Ever the eavesdropper. You laughed out loud. He heard you. Remember?"

"Well. It was that 'old girl' bit. You were seventeen."

He remembered the scene. He always thought in pictures, scenically. Even his ideas were pictorial. He'd stopped by for the first time. It was an intimidating pile on the edge of the city, leafy and out of trouble, beyond incessant noise. Her parents were older than his – well, there was only his mother. They were pleasant enough in that guarded, well-off way, the result, he supposed, of a heightened sense of loss and the need to conserve what had been hard won. If indeed it had been hard won. She seemed to belong there as part of their achievement – a lively, beautiful daughter with a future that must not be undermined, though they weren't overbearing; in fact, they were quite friendly, very friendly. For the first time he'd seen her in someone else's terms, seen himself as the person who might spoil everything. Hence the fatherly concern when he was returning to the sitting-room after helping her mother pour drinks in the kitchen, a distance three times longer than what separated kitchenette and living-room at home, three storeys up. Maybe his sense of scale was what made him an artist: big and small, grand and modest, aerial and grounded, discreet and obvious. The sitting-room door was ajar when he'd approached it with the glasses on a tray, tinkling to signal his presence. Her father was on cue.

He looks at her now, beyond her parents' death. She's more voluptuous than he recalls. What they ever wanted for her no longer matters. He never sensed that they liked or approved of him, but there was no outward show of dislike, just a reaction hanging in the air in case anything untoward happened. It belonged to people keen to have their unspoken or inarticulate feelings vindicated. There was a strong sense of that. Such people, he always thought, could never be fully known or understood.

He holds up the drawing for her to see what he's done so far, but she shows the model's traditional lack of concern, as though no response meant tacit sanction. He continues circling her, experiencing the old sense of privilege. He once told her that nudity, far from being a natural state, was self-revelation as far as it could go and beyond any point of discretion. In his figure paintings he'd always tried to convey the integrity behind the exposure, even where he suspects it does not exist. Such imposition of his own feelings on the thing observed represents a manner long out of fashion. But he perseveres, hoping there's something more than expressionistic to it. It's just like life: convergence of the self-possessed was always hard work, whereas taking advantage of a weakness, even to the same end, was easier and nearly always cynical.

"You were a deal older," she says. It sounds to him like a reproach, the cause of all that went wrong.

"'Grown up' was what your father said. Some fathers might have thought that to have been an advantage, a virtue – someone to take care of his inexperienced daughter. I was certainly sure of myself. But not so much now." He holds the sketchbook aloft. "This sort of stuff is *passé* these days. If I could get someone to video what we're doing, it could be exhibited as a work of art, given some obscure title... the video, I mean. The world's gone mad. The art world, that is."

"Conceptual," she says, immediately regretting the tone that reminds her of the little woman in timid occupation of superior male territory. At least he doesn't appear to notice. He liked models to show interest, share his thoughts.

"That's it," he says. "The triumph of the idea over the visual. Mind over matter. Some of it's OK. The visually-interesting stuff, I mean."

"Not an unmade bed."

"Definitely not an unmade bed. Or a made one, come to think of it."

"What about a crucifix in a jar of piss?"

"Possibilities. But shocking. More shock than possibility. Could a crucifix in a jar of human shit be considered a variation on a theme?"

There was a time when she thought such a conversation pre-coital, the model purporting to be the artist's dismissive equal in order that the subsequent leap on to the bed might not be one-sided, the taking of an advantage. She changes the subject.

"Talking of triumphs, do you see anything of Holly?"

"Not a dickie bird. She passed me in the street once. Didn't bat an eyelid. Maybe she didn't see me. And I didn't make myself known or attract her attention. Looked kind of sad. Why 'triumph'?"

"You always said there were no winners when couples broke up."

"It's true. What happened to Dave? Are you still together?"

"Dave died."

He stops drawing, lowers the sketchbook and looks almost affronted. He always complained that she sprang things on him. In their worst moments, he thought this a tactic, pre-empting his own inquiry or his tardiness in latching on to her feelings.

"Jesus Christ!" he says. "Why didn't you tell me?"

"It was two years ago. Suddenly. A heart attack. I suppose not telling you was deliberate. You and I haven't seen each other. We haven't been

17

communicating exactly."

"What was he? Thirty-five? Forty? I just didn't know. You should have told me. Phoned or something. I'm so sorry. Jesus Henry Christ."

She tells him that she and Dave were on the point of separating and that the flat they shared had become unbearable, meaning the sharing had. He places the sketchbook on a chair and is about to light a cigarette. He holds up the pack and asks, "D'you mind?"

"I'd rather you didn't."

"No problem. Even fags are out of fashion. I usually open a window. Look, tell me when you've had enough."

"Then?"

"I'll take you upstairs and show you some of my etchings."

She doesn't even smile and reminds him, without sarcasm, that there's no upstairs. He resumes drawing. She notices he still makes that odd sound of approval as work proceeds. A sort of 'Mmm...' noise inflected upwards. It had long indicated self-satisfaction. He never liked criticism so never invited it. He'd never had a lengthy review.

Then he asks her for something he immediately realises should have been volunteered. Maybe she was just waiting for the opportunity.

"Are you with anyone?" he says without raising his head.

She stares beyond him: "Yes. But we've... I suppose I grieved for a long time."

"What's his name?"

"It's Michael. We've..."

He's not listening or doesn't want to: "Did you grieve for me, when we..."

"God, that's a bit much, isn't it?"

He apologises in a way she remembers as meaning he's not sorry. She wonders if time's passing meant you only remembered life's bad bits, fearing their repetition.

"I'm sorry. You're right. You used to say I was crass, unthinking – insensitive. And me an artist. Contradiction in terms, wouldn't you say?"

"You were crass. You could be crass. Michael and I..."

"D'you know, I went to the National the other day to look at that Rembrandt self-portrait again, the one of him as an old man. Self-revealing and all that. And I thought, this could be a guy who's just despairing of old age, grieving for his lost youth. And it occurred to me that a wife-beater could do that, a rapist could do that. I could do that – self-portrait of a crass, unthinking guy despairing of his old age, grieving for his youth. What does he do – Michael?"

"He's a builder. Has his own company."

"Great."

She crosses her legs, oblivious of what he might think, beyond his censure.

"But I'm trying to tell you," she says. "We've finished. It hasn't worked out."

He scrutinizes her for a few seconds, as though he didn't hear, and then says, "I'm sorry. I really am. It's happened to me a lot since we... you know."

There's a pause in which she goes on posing and he continues drawing. They seem to be thinking about where this reunion might be leading, whether it'll soon be a matter of courage in not giving in.

"Is this a sketch or a proper drawing?" she asks.

"It'll be a revealing portrait."

"Will it be flattering? Will you show everything?"

"Of course. Inside and outside. The depths."

"Then can you tell?"

He looks at her, his head inclined, studying not the implication of her query but the way the hair is growing on the back of her neck, straining beyond the formality of her hairstyle.

"Tell what?"

"That I'm pregnant."

He stops again: "Bloody hell, you do have a way of coming up close. How? I mean when? Is it Michael's?"

She's not sure if impertinence, the reaction they'd once abandoned in favour of short-circuited if sometimes raw honesty, has returned. But there's an element of honesty she has to avow.

"I think so. I'm not sure. Can't be sure."

"Are you actually having it? I mean are you..."

"I know what you mean and the answer's No." There's a pause. "Are you shocked?"

He says nothing but folds the page over and begins a rapid sketch. It takes about fifteen seconds. While he's doing it, she gets dressed.

"I really don't know why you agreed to this," he says. "I've about finished."

"Call it re-visiting the past." She's brushing her hair: "Do you still make tea with that dreadful long-life milk?"

"Afraid so. But sod that. Let's go out. I need to think. We need to talk."

"Do we? Yes, let's."

She looks at the main drawing without comment. The rapid sketch is a broadly recognisable portrait of her, heavily with child, as the saying went, expressing the pain as well as the prospect.

"Will you come back?" he asks, rubbing his finger over the main drawing. "Would you like to come back

– you know, sit some more?"

"It depends."

"It always did."

"Lunch then. And we'll talk about it."

"Lunch. We've got lots to talk about. Have we got lots to talk about?"

"Maybe we could even…"

"Maybe. We'll see."

He allows her to leave first. He never used to. She distrusts chivalry, the thing he once said was 'not dead' though never exercised as part of his understanding of what he called 'the gender wars'. She wonders if he saw her disrobing as an attempt to show him she hadn't changed or had even improved – nakedness rather than nudity. Outside, she squints at the sky. There's a chill on the wind but Spring is struggling through. She remembers a holiday they took in Cyprus, almost dawn-to-dusk passion, and the visit to that museum with the drawing on ceramic of an aristocrat showing the upside-down baby growing inside her, making her plump.

She hails a taxi and he follows her in. She watches the passing crowds with a sense of accomplishment. There were some things he wouldn't get – the taste of metal on her tongue, the much stronger smell of turps in his studio, the bigger boobs, her nipples on permanent guard and aroused by what was inside, not yearning after something beyond her. She places a hand on his knee. "The dyer painting," she says, as the driver glances at them in his mirror. "What do you think it might mean?"

~

Nigel Jarrett is a winner of the Rhys Davies Prize for short fiction and the author of *Funderland*, a first collection of stories (2012) enthusiastically reviewed in the Guardian, The Independent, The Times and others. He's a former daily-newspaper journalist, currently freelancing, and he lives in Monmouthshire.

The Dyer's Apprentice arose in part from an actual event. Jarrett, a competent draughtsman – he designed the cover of his 2013 Parthian poetry collection *Miners at the Quarry Pool* – was working on a painting of a dyer that would stand as a metaphor for the artist, a lone and self-effacing character producing dazzling work. This grew into a fictional scenario involving a model who once had a relationship with the artist and is sitting for him again and reminding him of old times. There's a tragic element to it, and the story tries to say something about creativity and its necessary association with de-construction, with the scattered elements of what might have been.

The High Art of Bickering
Kay Beechey

"At this point, I don't want to mix art and science. Just like it's not good to mix friends and work and politics."

"'Onestly, Bert, you do talk some bullshit. What the 'ell are you on about now?"

I sit back in my garden chair and prepare to be entertained. Much better than daytime telly.

"You know what I mean," he continues, "You can't just slap it on."

"Bert," Molly replies with emphasised patience, "You're painting the fence, not the Sistene Chapel."

During their fifty years of marriage, my neighbours, Albert and Molly, have managed to perfect the art of bickering. Albert is the talker, Molly the doer and you know from the start it will be Molly that ends up painting the fence.

Albert, you see, went to Grammar School and got himself a "proper" education. He baffles us all by spouting Latin and quoting Shakespeare. "Pro quo vadis irritum" is one of his favourites. No-one knows what it means (not even Google) and it always makes poor Molly's eyes roll.

"For goodness' sake," she says whenever he starts, "Come down off your 'igh 'orse and join us 'oi polloi." Now Google did recognise that one.

As for the Shakespeare, my haphazard Comprehensive education and brief, uncomfortable brush with Julius Caesar means I can't really tell if they're right.

"You have to load the bristles properly," he says as he dips the brush into the pot. "Just the right amount of paint. No more, no less. And long, smooth strokes." A smear of fresh brown appears in the wake of his brush. "There, perfect. Not too thick, not too thin. That will dry evenly, you know, Moll. There's no need for a second coat when I do the painting."

"There's no *time* for a second coat when you do the painting."

Here we go.

Albert pulls himself to his full height and splutters, "If a job's worth doing..."

"It probably needs doing, so you might as well stop farting around and get on with it."

Molly snatches the paint brush. Albert storms off into the house. Oh well, that was a lot shorter than normal and there doesn't seem much promise of episode two starting anytime soon. I go back into my own kitchen and make myself a coffee.

An hour later I spot him walking into the garden with a tray.

"There you are, dearest." he says, "One milky coffee – just how you like it – and two chocolate digestives. Oh dear, you've missed a bit there."

"And you've missed the cup with the milk. We could feed next door's cat for a month on what's slopping about in that tray."

They sit down together on an old wooden bench that creaks loudly under their weight.

"How's the back, Moll? Playing up much?

"It's giving me a bit of jip it is, Bert."

"Well, you just enjoy your coffee and biscuits and I'll finish the fence, shall I?"

They exchange a look and I try to remember the

last time I shared such a look with my husband. A long, long time ago.

Half an hour later, I go back into the garden to get the washing in.

"Molly, dearest, I told you before; you can't just slap it on."

"I'll slap you if you don't leave me be."

I slowly put the washing in the basket then peg it all out again.

~

Kay Beechey was born and brought up in the South Wales Valleys, She says, I have always enjoyed writing. Although once a regular contributor to Walking Wales magazine, my first love is fiction.

The High Art of Bickering originated from an exercise at the local writing group. Kay says, 'The other members produced pieces in the twenty minute time slot, but I took two weeks to get mine together. Most of it was "written" on a walk in the Black Mountains when I kept hearing Bert's voice haranguing poor Molly. I scribbled it down when I got back to the car and finished it over the next few days.'

A Bad Date
Frances Hay

Tim's Date

The worst day of Tim's whole life began with a bad date.

He should never have clicked on that website. Louisa had a nice, soft voice on the phone and he quite liked the look of her freckled face and big grey eyes when they met up in Costa Coffee, but he should never have got mixed up with a divorced woman with a kid because here he was wasting a Saturday morning in the passenger seat of an old Ford Fiesta, listening to a reggae version of Mother Goose, heading out of London in quest of steam trains. It wasn't even as though she would definitely sleep with him, even if he passed the Thomas the Tank Engine test. And, by God she was a slow driver, but of course they had to take her car with its superstructure kid's seat and Tim had to pretend he didn't notice getting kicked in the kidneys by two angry feet in miniature Nike trainers.

After Louisa signalled for what seemed like years, they turned down a narrow, muddy lane, guarded by high hedgerows draped over with wispy strands of Old Man's Beard. Long thin green wands of brambles scratched the left wing of the Fiesta with their spiny leaves. It wasn't exactly raining, but the moist air periodically liquidated itself. Louisa turned the wipers on their slowest setting and shut them off again in tortuous sequence as they bumped their way through the potholes toward the Blackberry Railway car park.

If she always drove like this, no wonder her husband left her.

Louisa slammed on the brakes. 'Look, Benjy, look at those sweet little cars! It's like a parade of Noddy cars!'

'It's a rally,' said Tim. 'A Citroen rally. I've never seen so many 2CVs together in my life. Park over there so we can get out and take a look.'

'Oh, no, Benjy wants to go straight to see Thomas, don't you, Benj?'

But some primitive form of male solidarity kicked in and Benjy shouted out, 'No Thomas! Cars! Cars! Cars!'

'Good man,' said Tim, wrestling with the child lock to escape from the dingy Fiesta.

The car park was crowded with the French automotive version of a rainbow nation. Next to a turquoise model from the early 80s sat a blue-striped Beachcomber, adjacent to an acid green Bamboo. Beyond them were the mustard yellow model once driven by 007, a rhubarb-and-custard Dolly car, and a venerable cream number from the early sixties, its round headlamps on stalks like snails' eyes. Louisa chased after Benjy as he ran from car to car, trying to hug them all.

Tim stooped down to squint at the rectangular headlamps on an 80s-era Dolly, this one red-and-white checked like a tablecloth in an Italian café. Behind him, a woman's voice swore in French.

Inside his head, Tim swore in English. It was Yvette.

It was too late to pretend he hadn't seen her, when they were both standing on either side of a narrow Art

Deco Nile green Charleston.

'Teem,' she said in that familiar bored tone, as if they were still in the teachers' room at the Brighton comprehensive where she taught A Level French and Tim was learning he was the kind of person who couldn't either do or teach.

Tim had never seen a 2CV before he met Yvette, who had driven her miniature Citroen pickup truck over on the ferry. Ten years later, she looked as small and fierce and French as ever, in a brown leather bomber jacket over tight jeans, her feet encased in damp maroon plimsolls. She wore a flimsy silk scarf that on her, unlike most Englishwomen, didn't look like a misapplied tourniquet. She was smoking a thin cigar, its acrid smell cutting through the water-heavy Sussex air.

'Do you still teach there?' he stammered, watching her ash drop right on the polished bonnet of the Charleston.

'I teach people this and that. In France and England.'

But before he could ask her more, or, better, run straight back to Louisa and Benjy, two thuggish grey vans pulled into the car park, scattering rough chunks of gravel over the bonnets of the Charleston and Dolly cars, like savage mammoths trampling over the tin snails. Four figures leapt out of each van.

From behind him, Tim heard a happy squeal, "Mummy, look, Funnybones!"

The newcomers were dead men walking, their faces hidden by skeleton masks, their black jumpsuits painted over with DayGlo bones. They each carried long-nosed automatic rifles. In silent synchrony, they crouched down in the dirt like a firing squad and took aim at the oldest 2CV in the car park, an elegant sea-green Fourgonette from the 50s. Within minutes, the hailstorm of bullets had transformed the car into torn shards of metal lace.

Bullets ricocheted from the bonnet of the Charleston, at least one of them striking Yvette. She dropped down on the ground, her head smashing hard against the bulbous headlamps. Tim threw himself down next to her, calling her name, feeling for a pulse, but her open, sightless eyes were already dead.

All round the car park skeletons moved in pairs, one aiming his rifle at a car, the other extorting cash from its owner. "Pay or we destroy these fucking ridiculous cars," said an obviously Welsh skeleton. 'If not, we shoot you."

Tim wiped Yvette's blood on his jeans and sat up high enough to see Louisa backed up against the hedgerow, her right hand gripping Benjy like a vice. A skeleton pointed his rifle in her face. 'You too, bitch!'

Louisa dumped her handbag on the ground, then whirled round and shoved Benjy through the privet and brambles into the heart of the hedge. 'Let's play hide-and-seek!' she sang out. 'Run and hide!'

The skeleton hit her in the back of the skull with the butt of his rifle.

Tim lowered himself back on the ground, crawled behind the Charleston and a nearby Beachcomber, inching his way toward the hedgerow, toward Benjy.

Louisa's Date

Louisa's brain died in the middle of a bad date.

She should never have signed up for that lonely hearts website. Things were still so raw with Geraint. But she was so lonely. She'd never made the kind of friends in London she had back home, and after she moved in with Geraint, even her nicest acquaintances stopped ringing or calling round. When he left, there was no one to turn to except the counsellor at Gingerbread.

It would be so pleasant to go out with a nice, unthreatening man from time to time, maybe to the arts' cinema or even a decent grown-up restaurant: the kind that Geraint so despised, with bread soaked in olive oil and toothy fish swimming in red Welsh seaweed on oblong white plates. Louisa looked over the responses to her advert and picked the most unthreatening photo she could find.

Tim was not good-looking, not compared to Geraint's dramatic looks, but Louisa rather liked Tim's schoolboy cowlick and his sad brown eyes. She could be persuaded to have sex with him. But she wasn't ready for that yet. To slow things down, she'd invited Tim to the Blackberry Railway. This meant shifting Geraint's every-other-Saturday, so she had to tell him. He didn't like it but, really, it wasn't any of his business. He was so angry these days. Ever since he'd been going to those meetings of Fathers for Justice, he'd been banging on about his rights.

When it became obvious Louisa and Tim couldn't sustain a conversation past the London suburbs, she slammed a nursery rhyme collection in the CD player and let him sulk. She concentrated on driving through the wall of misty March air that never seemed to thicken into real rain. She turned off onto a narrow lane, negotiated her way around the bends as slowly and carefully as possible. The last thing they needed right now was for Benjy to get carsick. Long thin green wands of brambles scratched the left wing of her car with their spiny leaves. Sparrows darted in and out of their nests in the privet, cheeping madly. Suddenly the lane opened out and Louisa nearly crashed right into a bizarre collection of multi-coloured clown cars. Slamming on the brakes, she cried out, 'Look, Benjy, look at those sweet little cars! It's a parade of Noddy cars!'

'It's a rally,' said Tim. 'A Citroen rally. I've never seen so many 2CVs together in my life. Park over there so we can get out and take a look.'

'Oh, no, Benjy wants to go straight to see Thomas, don't you, Benj?'

But Benjy perversely shouted out, 'No Thomas! Cars! Cars! Cars!'

'All right, just for ten minutes. Then we'll go meet Thomas.' Louisa parked carefully and took Benjy out of his car seat, zipping up his anorak and pulling its yellow hood over his head. Tim had already bolted away. 'Hold my hand.'

The Citroen cars somewhat resembled Volkswagen Beetles, but were less pleasingly rounded, more angular and trapezoidal. Less like German kitsch, more like French theatre of the absurd. The cars' protuberant headlamps looked like snails' eyes. Louisa could see why Benjy liked them. They weren't serious cars at all. One was turquoise, another blue-striped like a kitchen towel. Several had two-tone colours like the saddle shoes worn by cheerleaders in American Disney movies. Benjy slipped his hand out of her grasp and ran from car to car, trying to hug them all. Louisa chased after him, trying to pull him away from the little cars. The mainly elderly, white-haired owners would not appreciate three-year-old fingerprints smeared on the polished bonnets of their most precious possessions. 'Let's try to find Tim,' she said to Benjy, scanning the car park for her lost date.

Benjy pointed and shouted, 'Tim!'

Tim was standing between one car that looked like a tablecloth and a green car that looked like an alien frog. He was chatting up a short, black-haired woman in a vintage leather bomber jacket.

So much for dating people from the Internet. 'Tim's busy,' she said to Benjy. 'I think we'll just leave him here and go see Thomas.'

'No, I want Tim!' Benjy ran toward Tim and the strange woman. Louisa had no choice but to follow.

Suddenly two grey vans pulled into the car park. Four figures leapt out of each van. Benjy laughed aloud. "Mummy, look, Funnybones!"

But the comic skeletons in Benjy's picture book did not carry automatic rifles. Louisa grabbed Benjy by the waist, lifted him up in the air, and ran across the uneven gravel until, with a piercing stitch in her side, she tripped and almost fell down. She crouched behind a little old car that looked like a pot of mustard. Benjy tried to wriggle out of her grasp but she clamped him to her side.

The skeleton army was crouched down in the dirt like a firing squad, taking aim at a very old car. Shots rang out like hailstones on a corrugated metal roof. The woman Tim had been talking to slumped down on the ground. Tim threw himself down on the gravel next to her.

Louisa grabbed Benjy closer and tried to edge along the hedgerow, toward her car. Pairs of skeletons wove around the car park, pointing their weapons at cars and owners, pocketing their wallets.

One of the skeletons pointed his rifle in her face. 'You bitch!'

It was Geraint.

And his craziest mates.

Oh, hell, the GPS on her phone. He'd followed her.

'I'm taking him, you fucking whore,' said Geraint, pulling on the hood of Benjy's anorak.

'Daddy?' asked Benjy.

'Daddy's in London,' said Louisa firmly. She whirled round and shoved the whimpering, thrashing Benjy through the twining privet and piercing brambles into the dark heart of the hedge. 'Let's play hide-and-seek!' she called, in the most normal mummy voice she could manage. 'Run and hide!'

Her husband hit her in the back of the skull with the butt of his rifle.

~

Frances Hay is an American woman who has lived in Wales for fifteen years. Her short stories have been published online by damselfly press, Persimmon Tree, Café Aphra and by Mulfran Press.

A Bad Date was written in response to a prompt in an online writing course. Frances says,' I was asked to imagine a scene featuring classic cars and to describe it from two people's points of view. I know very little about the world of classic car enthusiasts, but then I remembered a misty April day long ago when my six-year-old son and I ventured into rural Sussex in search of steam trains. We found ourselves in the midst of a parade of multi-coloured Citroen 2CVs, which drove their way into this story.'

Marco's Eyes
Jo Mazelis

His eyes are brown. Strike that word. Brown! How dull – like an old English teapot. Let us say instead polished amber. Or like the burnished breast of an African fertility sculpture. They gleam and reflect the light. Are salt-licked. Hungry.

His skin is copper-sallow. Taut.

This is not why he is famous however.

Fame. A word as hot as brown is cold.

Fame, he has it. Though it is not the fame of the Hollywood star, the actor in a soap opera. Few people would recognise him in the street, but put him in a New York salon, a Parisian gallery opening, in Harry's Bar during the Venice Biennale, a perfect Bellini kissing his lips, then you will see how eyes slide toward him, how strangers concoct first lines as they sidle up to him.

He has been my lover for one year, two months, three days and three and a half hours now. Yes, I am counting. Yes, I have a strong, a fierce sense that one day I will no longer be Marco's lover and that all I will be left with will be a few hairs scavenged from his pillow, the bill from Noma on which he wrote his telephone number for me. He didn't write his name on this which is a pity; a signature might have been collateral against old age.

I did not have to seek out Marco's company, inventing some excuse for speaking to him. The other night we were having an intimate dinner in a small restaurant in a village many miles from the city, but still, someone there, a man of around thirty years of age, recognised Marco – I saw his eyes open wider with delighted even faintly baffled recognition. He kept to his table, obviously (to my eyes) ruminating on an opening gambit. We had just been served our main dish, tiny Kobe beef burgers on tiny buns, with pickled vegetables, when the man who was terribly thin, terribly tall and terribly pale, came loping cheerfully to our table. 'Mr Scott. I'm so sorry to interrupt your meal, but I couldn't help myself.'

Liar, I thought, if you know you are disturbing us, why do it? Couldn't help myself indeed! If I stabbed him in the hand with my fork (he had rested the fingertips of each hand on the edge of our table as if he were at a séance and expected it to begin gently rising at any moment) then would it excuse the act if I said 'Oh dear, I just couldn't help it!' I didn't stab him and so he continued with his prepared speech.

'Mr Scott, I can't begin to tell you what a delight it is to see you. I am a huge fan of your work. You know I was at one of the earliest screenings of *The Rascal*. When was that? 1998? Then there was *Goat Eyes*, *The Red Barn Blues*, *Incarnate* 6 and of course, *Love*.

Marco looked up at me. I could not read his eyes. He blinked slowly, his fists seemed to tighten around his knife and fork, then he applied a smile and faced the man who had continued wittering on.

' ...and I suppose that this play between truth vis a vis documentary and artifice are signifiers of...' Here he stumbled '...they are a trope of erm...'

Bloody fool, I thought, perhaps he'll shut up now. But no, recovering himself, he went on.

'So, I suppose I always wondered... that is I wanted to know... if this... ahm... friction was accidental?'

'Accidental?' I saw a malevolent gleam brighten Marco's eyes – it was just as if drops of Belladonna had been administered. 'Oh yes, entirely accidental. Completely. Perfectly. Utterly.'

For a moment our interloper looked delighted, then mildly puzzled, then quite stupefied, then finally defeated and forlorn.

'I see,' he said. 'Well, thank you. That's...'

He stepped backwards nearly into the path of a passing waiter who had to swerve sharply to avoid him. Colour rose in his cheeks. Then he was gone. Marco skewered a floret of cauliflower, brought it halfway to his mouth and then thought better of it. He put his cutlery on his plate, pushed it away and sat staring off into the middle distance as cats will sometimes do.

I finished my dinner. It was delicious. Marco finished the wine, then another bottle too. He didn't pay for that meal. Neither did I. His untouched food you see. Accidental? Hardly.

I am the woman in *Red Barn Blues* and *Love*. You never quite see my face, it is blurred or shrouded or hidden by my hair. Or it is dissected in close up, my tongue wetting my lips, my nipple, the hot tip of my left ear with the light behind so it glows red. That sort of thing.

What was I telling you? Oh yes, how we met.

It was on a Greek island, a party at L-'s house. Of course it was L- I planned to seduce. Every woman there had that in mind. L- played guitar and sang some of his new material. He did that is, until some stoned English guy decided to play along on his bongo drum. Loudly, brokenly, entirely out of rhythm, but L- merely closed his mouth mid song and put down his guitar. The stoned guy, with his ratty sun bleached hair and his half-closed milky looking eyes, played on for some time.

L- was on the veranda facing the sea, a woman in a thin white cotton dress stood beside him, inclining her body towards his. She had long black hair in a tapering plait that fell in a straight line that emphasised her tilt. I watched as L-'s left hand came sneaking out and went behind her back and caught the plait and gave the gentlest of tugs to let her know he had her.

I wanted to know what would happen next, but then there was someone beside me and he said, 'Hey.'

He had this great black beard back then and he was as brown as a berry. What berries are ever brown? None, but that's the phrase, the cliché. The whites of his eyes were almost blue. And the irises were tempered chocolate.

I didn't have a clue who he was. I smiled then turned towards the verandah again. L- and the woman had disappeared. Maybe they went down onto the beach to make gritty love in the sand. Or they entered that warm moon blue sea. Or he led her to his room. Then there would be a song about her that *named* her. I wished heartily that she had some utterly unpronounceable name, one that was far too long to put in a song, that wouldn't rhyme and wouldn't scan. Bitch, I thought, and with that I turned to Marco and began to kiss him.

He first filmed me the next day. We'd taken a rented boat around the coast to what seemed like an entirely deserted bay. I'd undressed and he asked me to go under the water then walk slowly out and up the beach. I hadn't even got halfway to the water before this old woman dressed head to toe in black came tearing down the beach, cursing me in Greek, and threw a stinking old horse blanket over me. In the distance just arriving at the edge of the woods was the matriarch's entire extended family, daughters with babies in their arms, their young husbands, sons, cousins, aunts and children, so many children, toddlers, teenagers, eight year olds, five year olds, boys, girls, one set of triplets even.

I'm not sure how much of this he filmed, nor if he will ever use any of that footage.

He's been using a model for his new film *The Weight of the Water*. Fionnuala her name is, she's 22 but looks 15. Ginger hair, pale eyebrows, eye lashes that remind one of a certain pale orange insect's legs. Flat chested, flat stomach then hips – pardon me – that jut out and look like she inserted a wire hanger inside her. Not his type at all. And not exactly vivacious. Flat she is. No personality.

Marco has been my lover for one year, two months, three days, six hours, seventeen minutes.

He rang me just now. He's in Rio de Janeiro. We talked for nearly three hours. It's the middle of the night there.

The other day, I overheard him talking on the phone, 'Oh God,' he said. 'She is *so* superficial! Didn't notice at first but ...'

Fionnuala. Yes. Blank little Fionnuala with her cow eyes.

I deliberately made a sound then, pushing open the bedroom door.

'Glass of Chablis?' I said in a whisper.

He looked surprised, shook his head no, then crossed the room and shut the door in my face.

In his office he has screen grabs of Fionnuala all over his walls. She is predictably stark naked in a few. Freckles all over and dead white skin between the freckles. Her nipples are astonished rosebuds. Eyes green, but a sort of worn out yellow-green like grass that is parched and dying.

Fionnuala. He always pronounces all three syllables. It's never Fin. She's over there in Rio with him. She'll be all red raw with sunburn in between her freckles if she's not careful.

This wall of his used to be filled with pictures of me. One critic said, and I quote, 'His partnership with the female subject in Red Barn Blues reconfirms him as an exemplar of the unseen artist and his muse. Alone he is nothing, with her he is the very satyr of art – its personification.'

I did remind him of that when he was planning the trip to Brazil. 'Look,' I said 'Don't the critics expect me to be in this film? Don't you think it's risky? I mean, just when we're riding high?'

'We?' he said.

I shut up then.

Marco is paranoid about losing any of his footage – it's all digital these days of course, no more film gets ruined or lost in the lab or zapped by airport x-rays. So the rushes are uploaded to his cloud. I could take a look but to be honest I've seen quite enough of Fionnuala for a lifetime. And, well to be honest, I might just do something stupid like accidentally delete it all. I'm not so good with technical stuff as Marco knows. Unlike Fionnuala who was studying film at UCLA which is where he met her.

Sometimes we do things that we know are bad for us, drink too much, eat too much, take too many drugs. I sat through sixteen hours of rough footage. Stayed up all night. Did he think I wouldn't watch this? It's the first time he's appeared in one of his own films. There he is wending his way through the crowds at the carnival, coming closer and closer; he is looking directly at me. I know that face. I know that expression. He is ten feet from the camera, then five feet. Now his face fills the frame. His eyes might devour the camera. I know that look.

Marco's eyes are brown. Brown like cold coffee. Like shhh... Don't say it. Don't think it. Delete.

~

Jo Mazelis is a novelist, short story writer, poet and essayist. Her collection of stories *Diving Girls* (Parthian, 2002) was short-listed for The Commonwealth Best First Book and Welsh Book of the Year. Her second book, *Circle Games* (Parthian, 2005) was long-listed for Welsh Book of the Year. She was born in Swansea where she currently lives. Her novel *Significance* was published by Seren in 2014.

Of her story, she says, '**Marco's Eyes** won a prize in the 2014 Penfro short story competition. The idea behind it emerged from thinking about a certain sort of documentary photography where the subjects of the camera's gaze expose themselves during intimate moments in their lives; while undressing or in the bath for example. It struck me that once an artist has become famous for this sort of work they might attract friends and lovers eager to be part of their project as subjects and that their primary instinct is thus a form of narcissism. In this story I changed the medium from still photography to experimental film and tried to create a portrait of a relationship that was on both sides as illusory and fleeting as any art film.'

Dirty Corners
Malcolm Lewis

When Mrs Parry peeked out through the net curtains of her immaculate bathroom, Jenny Morgan was hanging upside down on the boundary fence, her dress round her neck, revealing her navy knickers. Downstairs in the scullery, Family Favourites was on the wireless. Evan Parry sat at the kitchen table with a pot of tea and two cheese sandwiches of his own bread.

Evan was a baker, with his own business. On Saturdays, he had nothing to get ready for the next day, so he finished early. Mrs Parry would have her elevenses later and had set aside an apple she would core and cut into segments. She was seeing to the weekly purge of her pipes, pouring caustic soda down the bathroom plugholes, but now Jenny's nonsense outside demanded her attention.

Downstairs she found Mr Parry, standing at the kitchen window, was also agitated.

'She ought to be in a home' Mrs Parry said sourly to his back, on her way to the kitchen door and down the garden path.

'Get down off the fence now. A big girl like you. Come on now, get down!'

Jenny puffed and pulled herself to sit precariously on the new trellis running the length of the boundary wall. It made the wall higher and was meant to make Mrs Parry's back yard more secure. But Jenny just found it good for messing about and climbing on.

'Shame on you, Jenny Morgan, shame on you. You should know better, showing yourself like that. At your age. Stupid girl!'

Jenny pushed herself off, landing lightly on her own side of the wall.

'Stupid girl' said Mrs Parry. 'You want locking up.'

Jenny, squatting down as if she might pee, scrabbled with one hand beside the path to scrape up earth and small stones. By chance, she scooped up a fat slug. She stood up, poked her arm through the trellis, and from her elbow threw the handful onto Mrs Parry's garden path. Looking straight at Mrs Parry, she wrinkled up her nose for a few seconds, then, as she ambled indoors, poked out her tongue.

Jenny, as people said, was a bit twp. She was simple minded. Now sixteen, she often sparked disputes between the Morgans and the Parrys next door. Naturally, it always provoked Mrs Parry to see Jenny clambering on her boundary wall, sometimes early in a nightgown, sometimes in only her dress, without shoes, socks or knickers. Or eating an apple, or a lolly, or hanging over the bricks above the lane door to reach and undo the bolt. Mrs Parry didn't know if it was just meant to rile her or whether Jenny wanted to ravage her lavatory, and garden, and perhaps steal her coal.

As Mr Parry was in trade, Mrs Parry set herself apart from the rough solidarity of the street. She had only the chapel outside of her domestic routine. Day by day, hour by hour, her pride, her passion for order, and her cramped sense of joy, sought their outlet in obsessive care for her house and her furniture. Her home was a shrine to order and hygiene.

From behind its windows, she watched the street as if it were a sacred site besieged by unbelievers. As its guardian and caretaker, its woodwork and furniture were polished and speckless, every wall and surface, indoors and out, was spotless and dust free. No dust accumulated above doors or doorframes, no dead flies lingered on window frames, no hairs ever remained embedded in bathroom soap, or blemished a plughole.

And it was her new indoor bathroom, the first and only one in all the streets around, that gave her greatest pride. The Parrys still used the toilet down the yard, just as they'd always done, though only in the daytime. But, there was no call now to use a zinc bath in front of the fire like a collier. Every day except Sunday, Mr Parry used the new bath, washed off flour dust and the potent smell of yeast, then afterwards Mrs Parry scrubbed and polished the bath, swabbed the condensation off the white walls and tiles, rinsed and wiped the floor, and rubbed marks off the door and woodwork.

It was probably unfortunate that Mrs Parry had any neighbours at all. Now, standing at the bottom of her garden path, Mrs Parry stood relieved at having seen off Jenny Morgan. Before returning to her bathroom, she stooped stiffly to brush into her dustpan the scattered soil that she then tamped down on the damp flowerbed along the wall. The black slug, creeping its way towards Mr Parry's lupins, she scooped up with the dustpan. She opened the lane door, stepped out and dropped the slug onto the compacted ash. She looked up and down the lane, went back in. Without thinking about it, she pulled and rattled the latch to check she'd locked it.

That afternoon Mrs Morgan and Jenny were doing the washing. So their washing didn't billow and flap against the trellis and to spare Mrs Parry any torment, Mrs Morgan had had Mr Morgan raise the clothesline. She knew that Mrs Parry would have seen him doing it, but she wasn't to predict the consequences.

Mrs Morgan had just rung out her bedsheets and pillowcases and returned inside when Mrs Parry called loudly from her garden.

'Mrs Morgan. Mrs Morgan.'

There was no response.

'Mrs Morgan! Mrs Morgan!' she called again, louder still.

Mrs Parry, standing in her backyard, could hear water running in the Morgan's kitchen sink. Mrs Morgan was in her kitchen and ignoring her. Not one to tolerate any kind of slight, real or otherwise, Mrs Parry rushed back into her kitchen. She clanked around in her cupboards for a baking tray, grabbed a large tablespoon out of the cutlery drawer, then charged back out, smacking the spoon against the metal.

Clang, clang, clang!

'Mrs Morgan! Mrs Morgan!'

'Oh my Jesus Jones' said Mrs Morgan, grasping the front of her rib cage with a wet hand. Expecting a catastrophe, she ran out into the yard. Jenny, excited, was right behind.

'Yes? Yes, Mrs Parry?' she blurted breathlessly. Mrs Parry, wide-eyed, glared back.

"You've moved your line, haven't you Mrs Morgan! You've moved it! Nearer the fence to drip on my flower bed!'

Mrs Morgan looked at the immovable wooden post holding up her washing line. A few feet from it, on the other side of the wall, the Parrys' post stood proud, crowned with an upturned bread tray to stop the rain penetrating and rotting it.

'Don't you try to be clever with me, my girl. All that soap. You don't rinse them properly. Mucky clothes. Ruining my garden.'

'What? My washing?'

Mrs Morgan was offended now, but it was Jenny, grimacing behind her, who butted in.

'Mind your own business, Mrs Parry!'

You go back in, Jenny' said her mam.

'Now!' shouted Mrs Morgan, when Jenny didn't shift. It was too much for Mrs Parry. She exploded.

'Don't think you can muck up my house!' she hissed. She marched out of her backyard and into the Morgans'. She stooped and put her fists round the stem of a lonely wallflower struggling in the shadowed scrappy dirt alongside the boundary wall. She yanked, but only skinned off a few leaves and petals, which fell away from her empty pat-a-cake hands. She tried again, tighter and lower, and the wallflower came up with the muffled pop of its roots tearing. She swung the plant round her head like a warrior with a hammer.

By chance it flew forward to thud into the wall of the house, the ball of earth and roots bursting over the yard. As Jenny, delighted, whooped, Mrs Morgan led her by the shoulders, up the yard, back into their house.

It was Mr Parry's emergence and prompting to go back inside that prevented Mrs Parry breaking up the hydrangea struggling in the corner against the Morgans' lane door.

He came back out to sweep up the spatters of soil. From inside Mrs Parry watched him through the trellis, sweep up, then trim away the broken

45

hydrangea shoots.

When Mrs Parry woke next morning, she could hear the well-oiled kitchen door bump in the breeze against the washing machine, but not the expected swish of shoe brushes on leather, nor the light accidental clunk of the polish tin on the kitchen floor tiles or the yard flagstones. Nor did she hear Mr Parry moving about the kitchen to fry bacon and bread and make a pot of tea. She looked at the alarm clock. It was too early for breakfast.

Through the bedroom window she saw the back door sucked to by the wind before swinging back from the doorframe. She didn't like the door left like that even if Mr Parry had only gone down the yard to the toilet. She put in her teeth, put on her dressing gown, secured it with a tight knot, and, in her leather slippers, went downstairs to the empty kitchen.

The open door annoyed her. As she crossed the room, the wind again pulled the door, lifting towards her face the long white net curtain hanging behind its rippled glass panels. As if it were a personal affront, she marched out the kitchen, down the yard, towards the lavatory.

A few yards away she heard the scrape of the bolt and expected Mr Parry to emerge. He didn't. When she reached the door there followed the sharp snap of the bolt hitting the end-stop. The door swung gently towards her. Mrs Parry, rooted to the flagstones, stared.

There was naked Jenny Morgan, wearing only fluffy mules, sucking a sticky lolly that she held in both hands. She leant forward from hips that had just detached from Evan Parry, sitting wide-eyed and rigid on the toilet.

With the quietest of moans, Lizzie-Ann Parry fled up the yard to the safety of her house. For seconds Evan sat stunned, oblivious, as Jenny turned round to him.

'She's gone. She gone!' Jenny said, pushing his shoulder. Evan stood, awkwardly pulling up his underpants and trousers, trying to tuck in his shirt.

'We have to go now, love' he said, buttoning up his fly.

Jenny stared at him blankly.

'We have to go, lovely' he repeated quietly. He reached for the nightdress hanging behind the door and held it so Jenny could slip her arms easily into the sleeves.

'Come on' he said gently. Arm raised, he showed Jenny out of the toilet and through the lane door. Pouting, she looked at him, then turned and ran though her back door, up the backyard. Evan walked away in the opposite direction, along the back lanes to his allotment.

As always after chapel and dinner, Mr and Mrs Parry sat in their dark living room in their personal armchairs, separated by the length of the settee. The wireless broadcast the Sunday afternoon Home Service. The moist smell of dinner hung in the air. Fatty local lamb, and overcooked vegetables – potatoes, soggy cabbage and swede from Mr Parry's allotment.

Mrs Parry was restlessly aware of the dishes and plates on the dinner table. Mr Parry slumped, tummy swollen from nervously over-eating. In his open mouth a dark strip of cabbage stuck to his teeth. Thinking about putting up a shed on the allotment, his eyes fitfully followed the lines in a western borrowed from the library.

Mrs Parry had already decided to do away with the outside lavatory. It wasn't in keeping. It was dark and musty. The gaps at the top and bottom of the door let in not only draughts and damp, but also snails, insects and autumn leaves that lodged in nooks and crannies under the pipes and outflow. The concrete floor and whitewashed walls were hard to clean properly.

The lavatory had to go, with the adjoining coal shed. Indoors she could have a clean gas fire. The garden walls would be tidied and built up, above the back-lane door, and on every side. She'd have high walls around an impregnable yard.

Mrs Parry stood up, carried the dinner things into the kitchen, and washed up at the sink in a plastic bowl. Like the debris she scrubbed off the pans, there'd be no trace left of the outhouses she saw down the back yard. She returned to the living room. At the further door she turned in Mr Parry's direction.

'We'll only use the indoor toilet from now on, Evan,' she said. Then she went upstairs to tidy the cleaning products and toiletries in her bathroom cupboard.

~

Malcolm Lewis is a freelance writer and teacher living in London. He has been a music critic for *Planet: The Welsh Internationalist* and a film critic for *The New Statesmen.*

Dirty Corners is set in a small town long ago when everyone knew everyone else, women scrubbed their doorsteps, respectable folk traipsed the Sunday streets and lanes, toing and froing chapel and church, and sex was snatched and often desperate.

Pocillovy
Susie Wild

*P**ocillovy*: Collecting egg cups. A word of narrow focus and specialist appeal, this is rare enough that no dictionary has yet opened its pages to admit it.

The egg cup had been missing for hours, days even. Its vanishing act had left the air in the new flat unsettled – muddled – and further disrupted by a flurry of activity as both occupiers rechecked the cupboards, the window ledges, and the remainder of unpacked boxes hidden under the bed. They recalled the last time they had seen it. There had been laughter and music and wine. There had been dancing, the shallow sound sneaking through the laptop's inbuilt speakers over the whirr of its engine; the man's samba moves causing the ceiling to creak in the empty flat below. The egg cup had sat, white and squat and strangely proud, on the dining table, dwarfed by the wooden pepper grinder beside it, the salt crystals held within its concave centre shimmering in the crooked candlelight. The woman had seasoned her meal, two small pinches scattered like ashes over her plate.

They were a couple in love and in the early years of still discovering. More so with each well-lubricated conversation and every post-coital pillow rambling; with each opened and emptied box hauled from storage at places neither called home – discarded hobbies and haircuts, dead pets and relationships. The half-lives led before this shared one. After years of communal living she now had a place to call home. Alice and Tim. Left alone at last in their first floor flat; their compact castle above the city. So far, so fairy tale.

Alice thought that finding the egg cup was essential to the health and survival of her relationship. Just as much as keeping the windowsill plants alive – the small heart-shaped cacti picked up on impulse in IKEA, and two flowering pots of pink and white offloaded from Tim's parents. She believed in superstitions, her own little rituals. She was a human Magic 8 Ball, since she was a little girl; a magic fairy, a sorcerer. *If I roll a six, Daddy will bring us chips for tea. If I wear my hair in plaits, Richie will ask me to the cinema. If I'm nice to Mum for a whole day, I will get an A in Chemistry. If the plants don't wilt, shrivel and die neither will our love. If he likes his meal, Tim will not leave. If I find the egg cup, he will come home.*

Her belly growling for breakfast, Alice opened a kitchen cupboard. Inside, the other white egg cup looked bereft, besides the two blue bowls, the pairs of large and small plates, the his-and-hers peanut butter. She couldn't bring herself to use it alone; she had her eggs scrambled if at all. Tim was not in the flat. He was often not in the flat. From Monday to Friday there was the office, which was not in the flat. Then he was pretty likely to be at the after-work drinks and the drinks after that... This time was different. A business trip away. Four long days and three nights alone and Alice had a fever. When she stepped outside the flat as night fell, the bright

Christmas lights made her feel giddy, she hallucinated; she would see Tim's face in bin bags and doorways; falling into patches of emptiness as the mirages faded. She missed him. Unsteady on her feet, Alice grabbed only the essential supplies – medicine, milk, yoghurt – for she did not have to play housewife this week – and fled back to her new home. Safely inside she shivered amidst all the undiscovered creaks and sounds, the neighbours' feet heavy on the stairs, the loud mannish shouts from the four Poles smoking in the garden, stretching their limbs outside of their cramped basement abode. Lulled by the hiss of the boiler and the fits and starts of the fan heater at her feet she thawed a little, additionally attempting to keep her chill at bay with the spare duvet, and ibuprofen caplets swallowed down with builder's tea.

Looking for the egg cup between coughing fits and nose blows, Alice instead uncovered old memories. She lingered over letters and photographs, lined up old snaps of herself, one in a Cornish harbour, one at night somewhere with the street lights glittering behind her, another with her hair hanging long down her back. She pulled her hand through her newly cropped do, nostalgic. Glimpses of her past inevitably led to others from Tim's. She was wary of looking too closely, after accidentally uncovering photos of his ex-girlfriend a few days previously. A woman who couldn't have been more different to Alice with her dark skin, tight curls and flat chest. A woman whose two-dimensional presence had sparked a row the night before Tim's trip. Alice shook her head at the memory, the sharp words, and hugged herself. She had been there before. For the first time in months she wished she had not quit smoking.

The egg cup was not amongst her pots of pens,

pencils and paint brushes, or under the messy piles of sketches and illustrations by her desk. It was not in the laundry basket, and the laundry was now loudly spinning itself clean in the washing machine, while she remained on guard in the flat, as stipulated on the rental contract. A lot was stipulated on the contract. Alice was surprised it did not tell her what colour underwear she should put on, or at what times and in what positions she was permitted to have sex or, among its many bullet-pointed pages, where the egg cup had gone. The hunt had escalated to the improbable now. The missing item was not in Tim's sturdy suitcase with their hibernating summer clothes. It was not amongst the recycling, hiding behind the washed wine bottles, or under the ripped envelopes and pizza boxes. It was not in the under-used microwave, nor the dirty oven. It was not lolling in Alice's lingerie or boxing with Tim's shorts. Sweat patches grew clammy – dank and nastily odorous in between her breasts, and under each hot, sickly armpit. She had to lie down.

She closed the curtains in the bedroom, shutting out a city disappearing into the twinkling cloak of night below her. The unmade bed was stained with sex yet Alice could no longer smell Tim in the room and not only because of the symptoms of her illness. He had been there. The patterns of his left-behind shirts clashed mutely in his side of the canvas wardrobe, and beyond, her mismatch of sequins and brights were slip-sliding from their perches. His pile of dipped-into factual books balanced precariously on the bedside table, underneath her box of tissues, open paperbacks, lidless biros, glasses of water, Strepsils and half-drunk Lemsips, but no egg cup and no Tim. He had been there, Alice told herself. Lying on his side of the bed she closed her eyes.

Alice didn't like to call Tim when he was away, her timing was always unfortunate – he would be going into a meeting, or out at the pub with colleagues. He would ring her later, he'd say, but he never did. By the end of the second day the loneliness hit her, and the worry. She would waver over the keys of her mobile, sometimes she would cry. Alice never called her friends at those times. She didn't want them to hear what she knew they would in her voice. She didn't want them to know that her new life in a new city with a new man was far from the perfect picture she had painted for them. They hadn't even met Tim. She doubted he would like them.

On the third day she opened the curtains in the office to find the pink flowers wilting, sagging towards the window ledge by Tim's desk; neglected. Beyond the glass, snow still clung to the path of the house opposite; weeping onto the pavement in the early morning sun. Alice pulled off the dead leaves, placed water in the tray, and moved it away from the ice cold window pane, the fierce winter bright. She muttered encouragement at the drooping leaves, the dropped petals. Hanging their entangled clothes to dry in the bedroom – shirt buttons hooked on lace knickers – she stared through the sash window to the city, frosty and clear below her, a sparkling blanket of rooftops snugly cushioned by strong hills. She gave in, scrolled to his name on the recent call list of her mobile. No answer.

Alice thought back to the night before Tim left – she could remember the silence, and then the awkward candlelit meal, but the later part of their evening of post-row reconciliation had become patchy. Tim had left for his trip quiet (and hungover) and the remainder of the evening, the early hours had returned to her in isolated snatches as she had gone about her day – some good, some not. In between the remembering there was the deliberate forgetting. The trying not to think about where Tim really was, not just at the Parisian business conference, but the people he was also visiting while he was over there. His son. His ex. Killing two birds with one flight.

Caught in the intense glare of the bathroom, Alice splashed water onto her face and leant her weight upon her hands resting on the basin. A tired woman stared back at her, puff-eyed and red-nosed. Bed-haired and crack-lipped. At her feet the bin was about to overflow with make-up wipes and toilet rolls, tampon wrappers and used sanitary towels. She left it as it was. It was easier to do that than to tell Tim each month that no, she was not pregnant and that yes she was sure. To see the second his face dropped before he caught it and pulled her to him. Before he kissed her forehead and held her tighter as their sighs escaped in unison. Her belly ached, long and low, like heartache, like loss. Every month brought a new period of bereavement, a red morning to mourn. She sank to the tiled floor and sobbed at her inadequacy as a woman, her barren salt-land of womb.

The cool white room calmed her fever and her thoughts. She sat there in silence for close to an hour. Just breathing and thinking. Breathing and thinking. It had been out of kindness that Tim had not put the photos of his son up in the flat, Alice knew that now. She knew that she should not have shouted. Kindness to their current situation and kindness because the baby snaps often included his son's mother, beaming, beautiful, complete. She wished she could take back the words she had said. She wished she were better able to control her temper when she was overwhelmingly upset, to diminish the inevitable regret. She figured, if she were going to sit there and wish for anything, it would be for her and Tim's wish to come true, a baby of their own, and a chance for him to do it right this time, a child they could love as much as they did each other.

She hadn't gone through the horror of tests yet. The doctor had been clear. Some women take time to conceive after coming off their contraception. It was nothing to worry about. In fact she really should try not to worry, that wouldn't be doing her womb any favours. There was more advice: *Don't blame yourself, don't blame each other. Do talk. Don't smoke. Keep having sex. Take a holiday. Don't try so hard.* It didn't make it any easier. All around Alice friends were filling up like balloons for a kid's party. Engagement rings were flashing. Christening invitations burst out of envelopes and beckoned her to toyshops for gifts. Successful career or not, she was beginning to feel more and more like a failure.

Alice had wanted to hold off, to not rush things just as much as Tim. She had had her share of hang-ups and commitment panics along the way. Yet now her inability to conceive appeared to be a punishment for the waiting. For holding off something Tim had already proved his prowess in. He'd got an A* twelve long years ago. Now she had to sit at excessive Welsh Sunday Lunches with his nieces and nephews, and that look his mother gave her, disappointed and expectant all at once. She couldn't meet it any longer. She made more and more excuses not to attend. Tim's son was a sworn secret, and one she would never ever break his trust upon, but the mother-in-law pressure had become too much for her to sit through for hours at a time. It left her feeling broken, useless.

A resolved Alice was on her hands and knees under the dining table, looking to see which nooks and crannies might contain her crockery, the still missing egg cup. As she peered into shadows Tim's parting words repeated on her. His rolling eyes. The deep sigh: 'Everything will be okay.' She had smiled weakly, meekly back at him and nodded. Reached up sleepily for a goodbye kiss, yet she had thought to herself that okay was not good enough, not even close. Alice changed her mind; after Tim had left the need for him to be right – for things to be okay – had engulfed her more each day. New illustration commissions had been ignored and old ones delayed. She had to find it.

From under the dark awning of the dining table her eyes began to adjust to the light, and Alice looked beyond the blinking green eyes of the wireless router, the sprawl of wires leading past the dust gathered under the towers of Tim's CD collection, the neglected board games and wrapping paper to the broken storage heater. She gasped. For no good reason that she could think of, there it was. The egg cup, lolling on its side like a drunk surrounded by a shimmering halo of spilt salt crystals. She closed her eyes tight shut, counted to ten and then looked again. It really was there. Relieved, Alice reached for the egg cup with her left hand and, as she grasped it, her favourite familiar sound registered; that of the key scratching at and missing the lock. Attempting it again and then turning in the flat door. She jumped up, happy, and knocked her right temple on the underside of the dining table. When Tim walked in she grinned inanely at him, his face framed by dizzying stars.

~

Susie Wild is the author of *The Art of Contraception* and *Arrivals*. She lives in Cardiff and has been performing her words in dives and dance halls since 2006.

She says, 'This story resulted from collecting new words, the contraception theme and my own lost eggcup in a new move. Addressing the adjustments we make to a new partner's emotional baggage, it is not as sad as it first appears. You can hear the tick of the body clock but also the growth of love. After writing it I researched the symbolism of eggcups and salt; together they represent a barren womb, the fear of the female lead.'

Pocillovy was first published in Susie's collection *The Art of Contraception* (Parthian Books, 2010).

The Big Send Off
Whyt Pugh

My complete lack of a corpse was rather inconvenient. This was my immediate problem: nobody I loved was dead, or even imminently dying. My parents are both very much alive and I don't have any siblings that could meet their demise under mysterious circumstances. I am completely lacking in terminally-ill grandparents; my mother's parents are happily (and unfortunately very vitally) living in Spain where I'm convinced their wrinkled skin is actually turning into leather and although I do have one dead grandmother this occurred some two decades ago and is therefore of no use to me in my current situation. My father's mother died when I was young enough not to remember and Bamps married a woman who truly believes she is ageing gracefully as Katharine Hepburn's long-lost twin sister. Well, whatever chemicals Glam Granny Beryl is injecting herself with they appear to be working for she stubbornly lingers on, a bit like Dracula really. I do have a few cousins going spare (car crash maybe?), but there is no way I could convince her that I am their next of kin, besides they're all kind of wankers so let them rot in their hypothetical ditch.

Okay, now don't get the wrong impression, I'm not actually a psychopath who would orchestrate the death of a relative, however far removed. It would just be really, really handy to have a dead body right now. This leaves me with only one option: I am going to have to devise a deceased relation, create a carcass, craft a cadaver. Not literally, of course, I just need to convince her that I have a body that needs to be buried. This is the part I'm a bit nervous about because I've never taken an acting class in my life. In fact, the closest I've ever come to thespianism was a certain DVD that my mate Ash smuggled to me in year nine and the title kinda rhymed with that, but yeah, nevermind. My first thought was to go to the swimming pool and float facedown for ages without any goggles on and think of what I was going to say, but the council closed the leisure centre. Cutbacks see, they must think fitness is overrated, let the NHS deal with that – it will come out of their budget then. Deciding austerity measures must be a laugh when you can drive your BMW to work out on your private gym membership. Saltwater then, it is going to have to be saltwater.

The shop had been vacant for months, but then I noticed a change, the whole village noticed. First, it was painted a sage green, very vintage, quite attractive really. Thinking back on it, I remember seeing her do it herself, but in those white and formless overalls over which pallet upon pallet had wept, I did not notice her. I am ashamed of that now, of how intrinsically society has written my idea of beauty. Then came the sign, each wooden letter carefully cut out in a curved and inviting feminine script:

The Big Send Off

Where people had been whispering before, now they started to talk. Most people thought it was a travel agent, some a party supplies store, but then, when the shutters went up, a collective gasp swept from one end of the High Street to the other: it was a funeral director's.

How irreverent they said, how tacky. The curtain twitchers and gossips said all sorts of things about her, but then two kids got killed on the new bypass and their parents took a chance on her and what she did changed what the town was talking about. It was beautiful they said – it wasn't really a funeral, it was a celebration. One young woman had been brave enough to ignore the idle rumours and because of that she had begun to dismantle the shell of grief that confined a shattered family.

Naturally, I was curious and so, as inconspicuously as possible, I ordered a portion of chips to eat-in at the cafe across the street. My reconnaissance mission, however, gleaned me little information and it forced me to draw up a plan of observation. To avoid being a stalker (and to prevent impending cardiac arrest) I knew that I couldn't go to the cafe every day. I therefore had to calculate what days were likely to have the highest volume of deaths and, in the absence of statistics, decided on Tuesdays and Thursdays as my uncle once told me that more planes fly over the valley on a Thursday than any other day. I know, I know, more people die in donkey related accidents than plane crashes, but there are plenty of asses in Aberbranog.

By the time I was brave enough to enter the shop, I had eaten enough calories of starch to rename the cafe Stiffy's Chippy. I watched her rub the arms of women who smiled through their tears and squeeze the hands of taut-lipped men as her fingers lingered on theirs in recognition of what they did not say. She never wore the polyester Victorian mockery issued to those in the mortician's trade, just a felted green coat with asymmetrical buttons and brown boots over tight jeans. She was real and I was trying not to admit that I was mental.

I had pushed my time of watching over plausible limits and was forced to open my theatrical debut without any rehearsal. I rubbed the saltwater in my eyes before I came into view of the windows and bloody hell it hurt. Luckily, when I entered the shop she must've been in the back room and so I had a moment to breathe and let the weight of my fictitious grief anchor me to my resolve. The room was empty except for four large banners suspended on stands proportionally split in two. I walked to the advertisement on the far-left and began to decipher the message:

Going Green?
Make an *IMPACT* in the right way
with our eco-inhumation service!

Leave the weeping to the Willows
with a made-to-measure
BASKET CASKET,
included <u>free</u>
when you select this package.

Um, okay. So does that mean you can recycle your relatives now? Maybe the next one would make more sense-

Voyage to Valhalla
Let your fallen warrior
sail into the afterlife

with this unique funeral plan.
Following the cremation,
your loved one's ashes
will grace the decks
of a scale model
wooden Viking ship.
Choose from a sea
or reservoir ceremony.
(Fire arrows and archer included)

I was actually quite intrigued by the idea and crossed
the centre divide to the third poster:

Sleeping Beauty
Give your princess
the fairy-tale funeral
she deserves with our-

"Hello."

I turned around swiftly, wide-eyed with shock and
saline.

"I'm sorry that I didn't hear you come in. I was just
putting the kettle on, would you like a cup of tea?"

"Yes, please, that would be lovely." Here I was,
conversing with her quite normally. Her voice was
measured, gentle. Of course it was – she daily
navigated the newness of those robbed.

"Milk and sugar?"

"Just milk, thank you."

"Please, have a seat in the consultation room." She
motioned to a doorway and I settled on a wicker two-
seater with comfortable cushions. There was a canvas
painting comprised of formless colours gazing down at
me. It had no frame as though to accommodate its
expansion as it swallowed my supposed sorrow. An

emotion I could not name rose in me and was suppressed; my pulse had increased dramatically by the time she returned with the teas.

"My name is Sam Sutton and basically I'm here for whatever you need or want over the next few weeks."

Damn, girl, I think that's a bit too generous on your part, let's get to know each other first...

"How are you feeling?"

"Numb. Afraid." You lying bastard, playing the vulnerability card.

"Would you like to give me some details about the situation?"

"It's my grandmother, she died two days ago of a severe stroke." Well, that is kinda true.

"When it happens without warning, it can sometimes be the most difficult to process. What I would like you to do is to describe your grandmother for me – give me a picture of grandma as a person."

"Well, she was one of those happy hosts. Her Welsh Cakes were the best in South Wales, let me tell you. She was a constant maker of sandwiches and teas, nobody went hungry. My grandmother always wore her housecoat for any task, regardless of the likelihood of the potential contaminant actually marring her clothing, but that is just how she was – a thorough woman, a woman of details. When my grandmother hugged you, her whole body and character hugged you – she was comfort epitomised." You idiot, you just described the most stereotypical Welsh grandmother ever, not at all suspicious. Why didn't you add that she washed the front every Sunday and reminisced about blacking the grate, tin baths, and coal fires with astounding frequency?

"She sounds like a wonderful, caring woman. What's her name?"

Shit, I should have known this was coming. "Um, Beryl." Guess glam gran was good for something after all.

"Was she religious?"

"No, not at all."

"Good."

"Good?"

"It is just that the absence of religion will ease my plan. It is just preliminary at this point and feel free to jump in if you have any ideas. I think we should celebrate Beryl the way she celebrated those she loved – with food and lots of it. A tea party, in fact, with little sandwiches. I will source a most delightful array of cups, saucers, and tea-pots. Leave all the decorations to me and the baking, all I need you to do is see how many of those infamous housecoats you can round up. How does this sound so far?"

"Uh, good. Is this for after the service?"

"This *is* the service. I believe in commemorating the life of the person, not focusing on the death. I want to encapsulate your grandmother as a person in a fun and unique way to honour *her*, not an archetypal construct of mortality. I am a funeral planner, like a wedding planner, not a funeral director."

"Well, yeah, that sounds tidy."

"But, you are right – there should be a ceremony aspect. I was thinking that at the tea party we can make candles out of our cups and then we will gather around the grave at sunset for a tea light ceremony. But, not to end on a sombre note we will return to the venue for a Welsh Cake baking and housecoat decorating competition. Will she be buried or cremated?"

"Buried." I didn't have any corpses to burn, or bury

for that matter.

"Okay, has the doctor released the body yet?"

"No, they want to do a post-mortem." Nice one butt, buying some time to procure a deceased volunteer to impersonate your wonderful, albeit non-existent, grandmother.

"That is very unusual as they know the cause of death."

"She was down the pit so it is compulsory." Stupid, stupid. Now, you've got a progressive pastry-making, pick-axe wielding granny undermining the institution from below ground.

"Well, well your grandmother is getting more and more interesting. Would you like to incorporate mining into the ceremony?"

"Oh no, she didn't like to talk about what went on *down there.*"

"Not to worry, I have no intention of disclosing her gynaecological records at the party." She smiled.

Don't talk about female anatomy, you beautiful girl, I can't concentrate.

"If you don't mind, Ms. Sutton, I would rather that I be personally responsible for all the arrangements pertaining to the, um, body like. I will let you know when she is buried." I am a master of deception, now all I needed to do was borrow a fresh, unmarked grave for about an hour. It is not like the occupant is going to mind, is it?

"If you are sure. You can always ask me for casket providers and things of that nature. Have you purchased a plot at the cem?"

"No, not yet."

"I have a chart of all the available ones. Should we go there now and you can select the one that your grandmother would have loved?"

"Yes, that would be lovely, thank you."

"Great. I will drive. Let me just go get my bag."

When she had left, I began to think that I actually might be able to pull this off. I tried to ignore the fact that I had gotten in way over my head and a niggling feeling of that something I refused to name. I didn't want to consider that she would eventually find out and then who would want to date a psycho who hallucinates super-grannies?

She popped her head back in and my philosophical contemplation was cut short.

"Shall we go?"

"Yes." I followed her to the road and got into the passenger side of the green Clio.

It was a quiet journey to the cemetery. I remember watching her with the husbands, brothers, and fathers and recalled that this was her man approach: emotion is not masculine, men do not grieve.

"I forgot to ask, how much do you charge for your service?"

"Nothing."

"Nothing? Then how do you live?"

"Well, if a family has a large insurance pay-out then I accept some money from them and many families give me donations that add up. But, for the typical family, I feel that it would be morally bereft of me to add the stress of finding money at such a delicate time. Death is to be treated with compassion, not capitalised upon. As long as I take enough money in to pay the rent on the shop, then I can continue business."

"That's good of you."

"It is not about me. If I can show people how to begin to chip away at the immensity of the boulder weighing upon them that is grief, shock, guilt, and regret, then maybe someday they will be able to turn that stone to sculpture."

This all made sense to me, but something struck me as a bit odd. We parked the car and began ascending the hill of proclamation where so many hands of stone rose tentatively into the air saying: I was here.

I have always thought the grass in graveyards was a more vibrant shade of green than anywhere else, as though the roots suckled and transformed all the intentions cut short by fire and locked casket lid. The late afternoon sun fell high on the quarry above, honey and slate from which all these people could have been carved. Even the heather stood starkly above us and cast a shadow too long for it to have possessed. As we climbed toward the vacancies at the back, Sam paused for a moment and asked if I would wait.

She made her way down the row of graves, carefully picking her way around each rise and fall as though her footsteps might disturb those beneath. Sam stopped at a small and indistinct marker, one that I would have overlooked had not the object of my infatuation turned her gaze upon it. From her pocket she extracted what looked like a glass pebble and placed it in a pot in front of the grave. She did not rise from her crouched position, but let her fingers taste each grain of stone. There was something so inexplicable, beyond tenderness or grief or love, in the mineral caress of her fingertips that I didn't realise until I was nearly there how I had been physically drawn toward the image of the stone woman.

I startled her with the clumsiness of the body that was too big for me and she shook the sediment of whatever I had witnessed from her as she rose quickly.

"I'm sorry," she said walking away from the grave, "let's move on."

She didn't want me to see the inscription torn from the rock that had survived glaciers, but I read as I followed her: *Seren Sutton.*

"At least you will get quite fit when you visit your grandmother, as all the available spaces are right at the top." She was flustered, trying to draw the attention away from whatever had died inside her.

"Are you saying I am not fit already?"

"No comment." She stopped. I stopped. "How about one of these spaces?"

"This could work. I would like to get a feel for the position, see if Gran would have approved. Do you mind if we sit on this bench for a bit?"

"Of course not, I need to sit down after that walk anyway."

The bench was cold and my already tense muscles contracted against it. It was also a rather small bench and I was very aware of how near my hand was to hers. The light had climbed higher into the crags and the grey of evening was moving over those mounds unmaking the molecules of the forgotten. I was drained of all I had ever been as I watched the coming darkness. Completely empty, I sat ashamed in the presence of someone who had spoken to death and turned back to life, volunteering to suture the irreconcilable. She was so much more of a person than I had thought possible, her pain was so perfectly polished. I didn't have those spaces within me to absorb any of her burden. All those things I couldn't see as I watched her from across the street I could see in the way her fingertips wrote her devotion in secret stone.

"What are the pebbles for?"

"Every time I help family, I put one in the pot."

"What will happen when the pot is full?"

"I will get a new pot."

The light was slipping further away.

"Sam, I don't have a grandmother."

"I know, but I still put a pebble in for you."

"Would you like to go get some coffee?"

From the grey she turned her head and smiled softly at me.

"Yes, I'd like that."

~

Whyt Pugh teaches at Cardiff Steiner School and lectures at the University of South Wales. She enjoys swimming with seals, wet moss, and intentionally getting lost. Whyt lives in the Rhondda Fach with her husband and their enormous white rabbit.

She says, 'I began **The Big Send Off** by considering the draw of observation; I decided to watch the watcher. I wanted to explore the sometimes comical repercussion of the extreme lengths one young man might go to in introducing himself to a woman who has intrigued him to clothe the serious theme of the work: death. Ultimately, I wanted to propose a village in which death was as individual as the deceased.

These Things Happen
Danny Shyla

You get drunk on Stella Artois, eat beans on toast and drink strawberry milkshake. In the morning you throw up and miss work. Your parents don't know you're still in bed – they never find out. It's your lack of energy for domestic chores that winds your mother up and dirty dishes in the sink that sets her off. It's a downward spiral: you're lazy; you're spoilt; you don't deserve to have them look after you.

So you miss work again, pack a bag, withdraw your Post Office savings and get a bus to the city. At the depot you read the *Advertiser* and find a room-to-let in a flat. It's on the docks' road. It isn't self contained and you share with a girl called Pelly who's Afro-Caribbean and speaks Spanish. She drinks tequila with lemonade and doesn't wear a bra. Her hair is everywhere.

You travel to work by train. The staff at Swanson Insurance are sympathetic to your situation because 'you're only seventeen' and they 'were seventeen once'. You lap it up.

Your job is to file documents and answer the telephone. Every morning you buy a pastie and a bottle of cherryade from the cafe and eat at your desk. You're always thirsty. You don't get home till twenty past six. Pelly cooks rice and peas for you. She doesn't work but wouldn't mind being a chiropodist.

Each night at seven Pelly changes her clothes, puts on mascara and goes out, so you mostly have the flat to yourself. There's only one bedroom and you sleep on the settee when she fetches a man back. You find a phone box and ring your parents to tell them you're having a great time. They say, 'We're glad to hear it.' They don't ask for your address.

Pelly takes you to a pub called The Exchange. She introduces you to a man with a hacking jacket and a beard, and goes off with his friend. Beard-man has wet lips. He buys you halves of lager. He talks about welding, and how he likes women with a 'bit of flesh on them'. You're seven stone five and he can see straight through you. When he asks you to go 'round the back lane' you say, 'No'. He calls you a timewaster and tells you to buy your own drinks. You don't see Pelly till stop-tap. She says, 'Sorry for leaving you alone.' The second time you go out she does the same thing – only this time the man has a scar around his eye. You wait for an hour, say you're going to the toilet, and walk out. Scar-man calls after you and growls when you don't answer. The next time Pelly asks if you want to go out you say you'd rather stay in and read. You miss your old friends.

One Friday night you catch the bus to your home town and walk into the local. Your friends are surprised. One of them shuffles up the bench so you can have a seat. They talk about how A level Maths is tough but English is piss-easy. They talk about eighteenth birthdays. 'You should have seen us after Roslyn's party last week. We were wrecked.'

You drink pints, which have no effect. At quarter to ten you say you have to catch the last bus. They say, 'It was great to see you. We'll come and visit you. Soon.'

At the bus stop you turn the corner and keep walking.

There's no reaction from your mother when she answers the front door. She lets you in but when you ask if you can stay she says, 'No.'

The last bus has gone, you tell her.

'There's nowhere to sleep,' she says.

Your bed is in pieces in the outhouse and she's given your brother your bedroom. Eventually, she finds you an old sleeping bag and you sleep on the floor in your brother's old room. In the morning you leave before anyone wakes. You didn't see your father. And your brother didn't come home. On the bus you count how many stops there are before the city. Forty-three. You get off at the station and spend the day looking in shop windows.

Pelly isn't in The Exchange so you go back to the flat. In the shared hallway the guy who lives downstairs is sifting through the mail. His name is Pearce and he's from the same town as you, well almost. He invites you up to his room for a drink. Asks you where you work, what music you like, if you've seen *Smokey and the Bandit*. You both love roast potatoes and both had pet rabbits called Bugs. It's cold in his room; he wraps you in a blanket that smells of cheese, and makes you coffee. You get hot and he says, 'Take your jeans off.' You really should go; you have work in the morning. He says, 'I'll give you a lift.' In the bare bulb light he has David Cassidy's eyes.

You're not sure how it happens but it isn't what you expect. You still have your shirt on. You're lying on the floor. His hands don't touch you. When he kisses you, you keep your eyes closed. You don't know where to put your legs and worry that he'll know it's your first time. It doesn't hurt. It doesn't last long.

You hear Pelly letting herself in; hear her keys jangling and a man's laughter. She lets the door slam. 'I have to go,' you tell Pearce. He lies with his hands behind his head, watching. Wetness runs down your leg and you blush violently as you put your jeans back on. He doesn't say anything about taking you to work and you don't like to ask, so you say, 'Will I see you again?' He says, 'Of course – we live in the same building!' You wonder if he'll kiss you before you leave but he's rolling a cigarette and doesn't look up.

For a few days you don't mention the encounter but when Pelly asks, 'What's happened?' you tell her. She says, 'What if there's a bebé?'

You discus names: Angelica, Mercedes, Julie. But decide to name it Constance after your mother. There's a shop on the High St that sells second-hand prams and Pelly has a friend who has a friend who had a baby and might have a cot. You will paint the corner of the bedroom pink and hang paper ducklings from a curtain rail. Pelly can knit. She will make booties and little dresses. There is no question that it could be a boy. The father is a blurred figure who passes like a shadow in the hall or on the path. You will work until thirty-eight weeks. You'll stop drinking to save money. In the summer Pelly will take her to the park while you do your job. The baby will be bi-lingual. She'll go to the Catholic school on the hill and learn to play the violin.

Pelly washes and irons your clothes and doesn't go out so much. She scrubs the nicotine from the walls and brushes the hair from the carpet. You buy a 'baby box' from the market and she lines it with wrapping paper. She finds a toy giraffe in a skip.

In work they wonder why you're smiling, and say, 'Perhaps she's got a boyfriend.' Pasties make you nauseated and instead of pop you drink tap water. You say you can't carry a box upstairs because 'you have a bad back' – it would be silly to take a risk. If they have a whip-round when the baby's born you'll open a bank account in her name. When you have stomach cramps you think it's just the baby settling.

The morning your period comes Pelly says,' Never mind.' You take the day off and she goes to the phone box, calls the office and tells them you're sick. You both feel drunk. You eat pizza and watch Kojak, then sleep in the same bed.

The bedroom has an empty space. A space that won't be filled with used books, cheap beer and knock-off cigarettes. On the way back from the pub one night, you steal a potted shrub from a neighbour's garden. And place it in the corner like a memorial.

~

Danny Shyla lives in the Back of Beyond and uses the people he meets on buses as inspiration. He studied Art and Design and plans to, one day, marry his words to his pictures. He is presently writing a novel and has ideas for several more. None of them are about sheep.

'These Things Happen,' Danny says, 'was inspired by a real-life event that happened to a friend of mine and I wrote it because someone needed to tell her sad story.'

Those Final Minutes
Gareth Scourfield

"Walk, always walk, never run," is what was screamed at us, but who in their right senses would believe that a person scared shitless would ever follow that stupid order.

For those final moments before we left the false safety of our trench, our confused brains screamed a myriad of electro-impulses to the rest of our shaking, quivering body.

Did any bone-brained, propaganda-believing idiot amongst us really believe that our fragile, imperfect frames could withstand the thrust and dash of skin-cutting, bone-smashing metal.

Pompous Lieutenant Orestone, he who looks as if he hasn't started shaving yet, is continually walking amongst us repeating the outright lie that we will be alright.

From somewhere a flare is fired into the air, explodes and the whole of this god-forsaken, death-ridden battlefield is exposed to all of us.

Is it a shocked silence or is it the evacuation of our stomach contents that has created us into being a company of mute soldiers.

"Three minutes to go men," Orestone manages to say, but how he has been able to say it is something I fail to understand.

A petrified glance from me, reciprocated by those on either side of me, and still he tells us to walk not bloody run.

I am assaulted by the sound of someone vomiting, followed closely by the smell of whatever it is he had wolfed down.

There is a change of mantra with, "Check your safety catch is in the off position and your bayonet is fixed."

Some shake hands whilst others just give a slight nod of the head to the luckless person next to him.

Another flare goes up – ours or theirs – but who at this point really cares who fired it toward heaven.

Battle police now stand behind us, revolvers in hand, to give that extra reminder to any who hesitate.

"One minute to go; take up your positions at the ladders," Orestone shouts with a quivering voice.

A shuffle of feet with the first to go over the top, already gripping their ladder.

From out of the darkness comes a plea from the heart, "Sweet Jesus, help me."

Men with bibles in their breast pockets, reposition them, so to cover their hearts.

"Ten seconds," Orestone shouts and his young, ashen
face is oh so obvious.

"See you in Berlin," someone says and then the
whistle is blown.

A scramble of feet and a tirade of machine-gun fire.

The body of Orestone falls back, dead, into the trench.

My turn to face Sister Death is here now.

The man before me explodes before my eyes.

I am showered by his body parts.

I smell his blood on me.

A something hits me hard.

My feeble legs buckle

I am gurgling

A light

No

~

Gareth Scourfield was born in Aberavon when the old
King was still on the throne, and after working in
Local Govt. for many years, it is only recently that he
discovered the joy and beauty of writing. He says,
'Writing allows my mind to go to wherever it wants to,

and often does.

'Over thirty years ago, the First World War found me. It grabbed me and has held on to me ever since. Many of my relatives fought in that war, including both my grandfathers and many great-uncles. I am aware of some of their stories. All of the servicemen who struggled with tensions, privations and even hopes for the future, inspire me to write about them, albeit in a fictional way. On visits to the Western Front battlefield areas, I have stood in actual WW1 trench lines. On one of those occasions, I wondered what I would have felt or said or done if I had been in that trench, preparing to leave its false safety, as part of an attack on the enemy. My story, **The Final Moments** comes from my thoughts of what it might have been like. Its format of the first line of the story being 30 words, the second 29 and so on until the final line of one word, came from a writing prompt from someone who I now like to call a friend.'

Valse Musette
Elizabeth Morgan

It was late summer. The midday sun was still hot, though not as intense as in past weeks. The square in the centre of Avignon was full of foreign visitors, and a cacophony of languages jostled with each other, as sun drenched bodies worked their way through the dozens of café tables sprawled across most of the pedestrian area. Some gave up the struggle, succumbed, and sat down.

Heat, combined with the seductive aromas of a Provencal dejeuner, was too much. Several waiters from adjacent cafés circulated amongst the tables, bearing shoulder high their offerings.

Somewhere, in what appeared to be the centre of this melee of tables and people was a clearing; a large open space. Here a young man stood, alone, quite apart from the rest, with an accordion slung across a shoulder. No one seemed to take much notice of him, nor he of them. In fact, after about ten minutes he sat on a tree stump, the only piece of natural vegetation preserved in this urban development. If this was Avignon's answer to St Mark's, we needed an orchestra surely. But all we had was a young man and a silent accordion.

The noise from the tables however made up for the lack of musical accompaniment, except perhaps for the one nearest to me, on my right. There sat a lugubrious middle-aged man, silent and alone. When the waiter arrived with his meagre salad platter, meagre that is for a dejeuner in the Midi, he barely nodded a response. He was dressed in the uniform of a French government bureaucrat, a short sleeved blue shirt, and grey trousers. On the table lay a flat briefcase. From time to time, he jotted down notes on the back of a Gitane packet. His eyes, brown and rheumy, were fixed on some distant point in time and place. During all the events, which followed, that afternoon in Avignon, his face remained immobile, impassive, his eyes saw nothing, his ears appeared to hear nothing.

On the other side was a table of four lively young people, Danish I thought. They were bronzed, and bouncing with high spirits. The two boys, dressed in shorts and tee shirts were blond and handsome, their teeth dazzling white against tanned faces. One girl, the dark one, with a pert lively face, was recounting a story that was arousing much laughter from the group. The other girl a delicate slender little blue eyed blonde of about twenty, was also amused, but appeared to be shyer, less extroverted than her dark companion. For like the lugubrious neighbour, her eyes reached out to some distant point in time and place. The storytelling was interrupted by the waiter arriving with plates of jambon, and pommes frites, and the four fell to, with eager appetite.

Further away sat a table of heavy Germans, swilling lager and laughing loudly. One of them was considerably older than the rest, old enough to have been here during the war. As he was pointing out places of immediate, and local interest, he probably was.

In the other direction a pair of pale, wispy English ladies were quietly sipping their infusions. Certainly their colour had not changed since leaving England, despite the sunshine. They wore large straw hats, the uniform of certain British in the sun, silk blouses, and Liberty print skirts, which would have suited Knightsbridge as admirably as they now graced Avignon.

Without warning, as if from a secret signal, the accordionist jumped up, and slung the instrument across his chest. I looked at my watch, it was 12.30 pm.

The music started, unmistakably French, playing all the old melodies that generations of Francophiles have loved and will continue to love. Out they tumbled from his nimble fingers; *Louise, La Mer, La vie en rose.* He played well, but no one seemed to take much notice, and even when he stopped after a particular selection, few bothered even to put down knife, fork, or glass, to applaud.

The German table enjoyed the *Pasodobles*, for they thumped out the rhythm with the palms of hands, and almost succeeded in knocking over a couple of beer glasses causing much merriment.

Now came the turn of the *Valse Musette*. I do not think there is any sound that captures the essence of the romantic's Gay Paree, more than the *Valse Musette*. Its sound spans those years from the turn of the century to the outbreak of the Second World War when Paris, was Queen of cities; the unrivalled Mecca, to whose gates, artists, writers, and sophisticates made their pilgrimage And of course those in search of a holier grail, the disciples of l'amour, in all its forms – sensual, lecherous, loving, lonely, forbidden, exciting, naughty. How many English maidens had come to Paris in search of it; found it, swooned with delight, whilst it wreaked havoc with maidenly virtue, but who were finally obliged to leave it, broken hearted, to return to Mama and a sensible marriage in England.

I looked at the two English ladies. Had they? Their faces gave little away.

Suddenly, there she was, in the clearing with the accordionist, her feet moving lightly and expertly as she followed the rhythm of the valse. How and when she arrived there, I shall never know, this thin small scrap of a woman. She was well into her seventies, dressed in a badly cut navy blue skirt, white blouse, and a bright blue cardigan, which hung about her narrow shoulders and hips, like a sack. Her hair was unevenly dark, snow white at the temples. Thin strong legs, and dainty little feet, clad in dancing pumps, propelled her nimble frame round the musician. She wore thickly powdered makeup, with two pencilled eyebrows, expertly arched. High on her cheekbones, rouge had been dabbed, and two bright red streaks, badly smudged were drawn across lips that had once known the fullness of youth.

The English women pretended she did not exist, for clearly she embarrassed them. It is odd about the English; those whose behaviour is not of the adult norm, whatever that may be, should always be ignored. To regard, to observe, is merely to encourage 'showing off', and this is to be discouraged at all costs. Making an exhibition in public is nothing less than a sin.

The Germans found her a figure of ridicule. From time to time, one of them would make a remark, bringing heads together bowed low on the table. Then there would be an explosion of laughter; heads, bodies, arms, thrown backwards, teetering on spindly chair legs, sometimes so loud as to drown the music.

The three young Danes regarded her with that kindly air of patronage that the young, on occasions, mete out to the old, an indulgence that is usually reserved for children. The pretty young blonde however appeared completely captivated by the old danseuse. She watched every step, every gyration, her eyes large and unblinking, as though mesmerised.

When we are young we can never imagine ourselves growing older; it is absurd, unthinkable. And though it is plainly an undoubted fact as life progresses, it remains nevertheless just as unacceptable as when we were twenty. For is that not nature's wickedest piece of witchcraft; that trapped inside our decaying physical forms, is forever the spirit of a twenty year old? I believe for those moments, the pretty young blonde understood that, completely.

The accordionist now slowed his tempo slightly, as he went into one of the really evocative valse musettes, I think it is called *Valse Grise*. It has a haunting, nostalgic quality, which took immediate effect upon the old danseuse.

She stood quite still for the briefest moment. Then she wrapped her arms about her frail shoulders, smiled, closed her eyes, and began to sway gently from side to side.

Gradually her feet began to respond to the haunting melody, but so lightly, and with great delicacy, as though the very air through which she passed, were made of such fragile substance, any sudden movement could rend it apart. She opened her eyes, seeing what we could not. She was transported into another time, another place. Out went her arms in a graceful gesture, drawing close to her body an imaginary partner. Imaginary? Not to her. For dancing with someone she certainly was. Her arms moved tenderly to his shoulders, her hands about his neck. She would smile; turn shyly, head to one side, as though sharing a whispered confidence. The music quickened its pace. Her hands slipped down to his waist. Faster and faster played the accordion, faster and faster the old danseuse moved until she was spinning round and round, eyes shining, head thrown back, laughing with her phantom partner, her hands still clasped about his waist

Until that moment I had always believed that beauty was the prerogative of youth. The rest was simply a process of diminishing returns, body and mind. But in the face of this old woman, I saw beauty. A beauty that shone from her twenty year old spirit, no more trapped within a decaying frame, but released, and shining through her eyes, her smile, her every gesture, as she relived a memory, undimmed by the passage of time.

Though tears were now filling up her large eyes, the young blonde was smiling. How could she not, witnessing such unabashed joy.

She understood.

Her friends seemed not to notice, for they were by now deeply into discussion, their backs to the clearing.

The accordionist burst into a frenzied finale, but the old danseuse matched him, step for note. She spun dizzily, feet moving at a blurring speed, until the final stupendous climax, and the accordion was drawn out for the closing chord. The danseuse stopped, radiant, smiling, as she took her curtsey, deep, low, head held high with childlike charm, to one side. Few people bothered to applaud. The Germans did, loudly, and laughed as though this was the funniest thing they had seen since Charlie Chaplin. The young blonde clasped her hands together in a gesture of applause, but instead wiped the tears from her cheeks. The lugubrious neighbour who had seen nothing was still jotting down notes on another Gitane packet.

My attention being thus taken away, I did not see clearly what happened next, but in an instant it would seem, the old danseuse was lying on the ground. She had obviously keeled over after her graceful curtsey. The accordionist ran to her, and tried to lift her up. Gently he laid her on her back, and put his folded jacket under her head.

She was still smiling.

A few people murmured. The English ladies looked pained, shook their heads knowingly in a 'this is what comes of showing off' gesture and called the waiter for their bill. The manager and an acolyte ran to the motionless figure. He lifted a limp arm, felt her pulse, and shook his head. A blanket was found from somewhere and laid across her body. By now a few people had left their tables, craning to get a better view. One client, obviously a doctor, knelt by her side, and put his ear to her chest. He too shook his head.

The Germans left abruptly. This was taking a joke too far.

The blonde Danish girl buried her head in her folded arms resting on the table. Her friends looked at each other, bemused and puzzled.

I stood up, and prepared to leave, for there was nothing one could do under the circumstances. As I took a last look at the motionless form of the old danseuse, lying, childlike in its diminutive proportions, arms and legs stretched out, I noticed her face.

The smile was still there.

Minutes later as I walked through the town, I

heard the wail of an ambulance siren as it sped towards the café in the square. Strangely, I did not feel I had witnessed a death, but rather the closing number of a theatrical entertainment. For us, the curtain comes down, but do we ever doubt the continuing activity back stage?

Surely death does not smile.

But was the smile in death, or after death?

Had she finally been united with him, her partner?

The one with whom she had danced, so perfectly, her last Valse Musette?

~

Elizabeth Morgan is an occasional director and lecturer, but mostly actor and writer, playing in TV radio and theatre over many years plus writing over 34 performed plays covering all media, short stories in collections, two books on France and two novels.

Of **Valse Musette**, she says,' I was in Avignon, a stunning medieval town, but as I am an ardent Francophile to me the whole country and its enchanting idiosyncrasies, are equally lovely.

It was a hot sunny day, and I strolled into the main square sprawling with tables belonging to the encircling cafés bistros and restaurants. I clocked the surrounding tables and their occupants while waiting for my coffee. The accordionist was in the square sitting on a large ornamental stone, and he began playing to his quiet mumbling audience. Then the tiny little figure appeared and she began to twirl delicately and with a practised skill to the familiar music, while I watched the reactions of the surrounding clientele . Most fiction is nudged into life by reality, an incident, a story, the rest is creative imagination in turn fired into action by the writer's constant question, What if? And therein lies the creative process. How much or how little of the original incident remains in the completed work, as readers we rarely know, nor even care.'

Thick
Lynda Nash

'Why d'they call you Rob?' she asks.
'I robbed a bank.'
She giggles. 'You're having me on.'
'Can't get anything past you... it's because I look like Robert De Niro.'
She squints, turns your head profile on. 'Maybe. Just a little bit...'
Women like it when you lie to them. The truth is so much less, so average, so normal. They don't sit on barstools for normality.
You fumble in your wallet for a tenner to pay the barman. The note is caught in the stitching. 'Here, let me.' She hooks a long, painted fingernail under the flap and drags the note free. You'd have crumpled with embarrassment once but the years have neutralised your feelings – plus you had a few before you got here. Deftness isn't your strong suit. You weren't a dexterous child, your fingers too thick to steer a pencil or master an instrument. Like playing the piano with sausages, your music teacher said. Robirch became your nickname. Rob for short.
Her name is Sheila and her 'absolutely favourite film of all time' is *Meet The Fockers* or so she says. 'Made me pee my knickers the first time I saw it.' She thinks De Niro suits comedy. 'It's his deadpan expression that does it.' You consider dropping the De Niro line having no real interest in the guy yourself.
She crosses one bare leg over another and you get a

glimpse of inner thigh under her thin denim skirt. 'Who would you like to play you?' she asks. 'You know, in the film of your life. I'd like Dolly Parton or Madonna, or maybe that girl from the shampoo ads, she could play a younger me. I used to be that thin when I was twenty-something. Kids, that's what does it.' She lifts her top and prods her stomach. You see a trace of a brown line running from her belly button into her pubes that suggests she's not long popped one out. 'Should never have had kids. Kids ruin your figure. Unless you're a man, of course.' She laughs, looking at you, expecting you to join in. But you won't. Why should you? You want company not comedy.

You order another round. The barman pours a beer and a gin and tonic, watches Sheila jab a slice of lemon with a straw. He's got his eye on her you think. Perhaps he's had her. 'No calories in gin,' she says. 'Gotta be careful, what with all this talk about obesity and junk food.' You wonder if she classifies alcohol as a food group.

She strokes your hand, her fingertips like sandpaper. 'Your fingers aren't all that fat,' she says as if in response to an unspoken question. 'I can do a lot with them,' you say. She drifts off, probably visualising your fingers inside her: one finger, two, three. 'Depends how wide it is,' you say. She says, 'Uh?'

It's only half ten and Sheila's so dull you'd rather be at home reading Carver and waiting to die. You need some spark of intellect or you'll never get it up. You're thinking of an excuse to leave when she says, 'Men don't like me, you know. Well one did, obviously, because he gave me William and Hannah, but before and after him, well, you know. Anyway I don't mind living alone. I've got Joe. I get in and you should see him all waggy and yappy and jumping up and laddering my tights. I named him after Sly Stone in *Throw Momma from The Train*.' You don't tell her she's got the wrong film. 'The amount of tights I go through...but when I see that cute little mutt with his drippy jowls I forget the world isn't all it's cracked up to be. He's my rock.'

'What happened to him?' you ask.

'He's back at mine, flat on his back making little snuffly noises like he's ...'

'The guy, your ex-husband.'

'Ha, we weren't married.' She sighs. 'He didn't want to rush things. Then the silly bugger went and shot himself... with a rifle, you know one of those with a bayonet on the front. Not on purpose, mind you, just one of them freak accidents... he always used to tell me I had body dysmorphia...' Her fingers tighten around her glass and for the first time since you got here you look at her face, actually look right at it. The channels around her mouth, the yellow tinge to her skin, the grey-white of her eyes, the crooked tooth that's losing its enamel...

'You're pretty,' you say, though you don't think you mean it.

'Nah,' she says and shrugs. 'You know, when I was a kid, pubescent and all that, I wanted buck teeth and glasses. I thought beautiful girls had buck teeth and glasses. Like Carrie Osborne. She had a different boy every week. They were queuing up to take her out. I wanted that. I was flat as a pancake then.' She sticks out her chest. 'But it was the teeth that did it. And the winged frames. Well I got one of them at least...' She digs in the bag that's been on her lap since she sat down and pulls out a pair of specs with lenses as thick as jar bottoms but doesn't put them on. 'I don't bother to wear them when I'm working,' she says. 'I don't need to see who I'm doing.' She strokes the length of your fingers one by one, slowing to pay particular attention to my ring finger. 'Most blokes are too impatient to even buy me a drink let alone talk, but you seem different...'

~

Lynda Nash was born one summer but not in a garden. She teaches English the creative way, has had a few books published and is writing a novel for her PhD. You can find her at **lyndanash.co.uk** or at home playing Killer Suduko and thinking about writing.

She says, '**Thick** was born in my garden, last summer, when the words "fingers like pork sausages" popped into my head and I grabbed paper and pen and started writing.

Taking Shape
Christina Thatcher

When Emma was young, before she grew taller than the sunflowers on Hanover Street, she would sneak out the back door of the house to peek at her father's foundry. It was an old place full of half-hushed stories. Even the yard outside was filled with cracked clay and bronze that had broken off the bells as they passed in and out of the foundry. When her mother wasn't watching, Emma would crouch down and pick up the remnants the bells had left behind. She liked the bronze pieces best; they were smooth, rare and still held onto their shine.

Although she tried to be quiet in the yard, Emma sometimes got caught with clay on her hands. In a calm voice her mother would remind her that she was never to go to the foundry or foundry yard because it was dangerous. She said that it was not "for little girls or young women." Emma knew that bells were a man's world; she had heard her mother say it hundreds of times. Emma could not understand this other world, the world of men and bells; she only knew that the bells were *her* world and that she loved them.

When Emma began school she cried. Not because she hated leaving her parents but because she hated leaving the bells. During morning classes Emma read beneath her desk, filled notebooks to the brim with blueprint drawings of hand bells, church bells, and tower bells. By midday she'd research bronze and alloy, copper and tin, zinc and brass, and imagined their weight, feel, and texture. And, after she got home and ate dinner, she would sneak out to tell the bells what she had learned.

As the years moved on she made her way from words to drawings. At first her pencilled bells had looked something like triangles, stiff and rigid, but soon Emma understood the curve and her bells looked more like supple bodies. She was proud of what she knew.

By the time she started bleeding she knew the ins and outs of every bell there was to know. But that same year, in the belly of July, the light was snuffed out in the Ainsworth Foundry. Emma's father, who had overseen his world for 40 years, had become ill, with "Bell Lung", her mother called it. She said it was like "Black Lung", the disease that plagued coal miners when they'd spent too much time in the earth, but instead of inhaling coal and rock and dust Emma's father had inhaled too many shavings of bronze and clay. Emma wondered if his lungs, instead of being black, looked like small, bronzed sculptures. She cried when the lights went out and every night thereafter; she could hear the tradition dying every evening in the phlegm-filled coughs of her father.

To soothe her heart and mind after the foundry was locked, Emma made frequent trips to the yard to sit beside the bells. Her mother was tending her father so she could sneak out easily. Emma felt she was old enough, and knew the bells well enough, to touch them. She would sit calmly alongside each one and stroke their curves, palm first to feel as much of the damp bronze as she could on the body, then fingers over the cast inscriptions. When she stood up she would press the corner of her hip and the top of her shoulder against each one and together the space between her and the bronze would form a long oval. She could measure the curves of the bell against her own and form rounded shapes; she was growing up and into something.

The next year left deeper coughs, taller curves, and cobwebs in the foundry windows.

On the anniversary that the lights went out, Emma sat barefoot with the bells and a key. She had crept in and taken it from her father's bedside table after he had coughed himself into exhaustion and after her mother had drunk herself to sleep. The key was heavy and cool in her slender hands. Her mother had told her the foundry was an oppressive place, small, confined, muggy. It was a place of muscle and brawn. Still, Emma longed to be enveloped, to pull all of it inside herself.

As she stood up and walked towards the foundry door, she took slow, deep breaths through her mouth and nose. Her expanding lungs stirred her heart to beat and her stomach to churn. The bells sat silently. Nothing was disturbed by Emma, no blade of grass or broken clay. She moved as though she were the yard, yet belonged within the foundry.

When she reached the door, Emma pushed the key into the lock and turned. She felt the weight of it catch and unlock the door that had stood between her and the foundry – the man's world and the lonely bells – since her childhood. She closed her eyes, pressed her shoulder against the wrought iron front, and pushed, sliding the heavy door open, then shut.

When she opened her eyes the dust stuck to them Emma rubbed until the tears came. It was night, but she did not turn on the lights; the moon flared in through the windows so that she could see the world.

Like the yard, the corners were filled with bells. In one, lived large tower bells that had turned a deep green colour from the years they'd spent singing in Cathedrals. They were waiting to be restored. In another corner, there were newer bells, ones her father must have made before he closed the foundry. In the last two corners there were moulds, and casts, and founding equipment. It all sat empty, waiting to bear new bells. She could feel the heat of this place. The sweat of the summer hung along the walls. She could taste the clay on her tongue. She breathed everything in deeply until her lungs and diaphragm expanded, then she exhaled. It was just as she'd imagined it.

Emma spread her toes and moved with the balls and heels of her feet gracefully along the ground. The bronze shavings were soft, like cottoned dust. They covered her feet as she walked toward the tower bells. She slid down along the wall, pulled her legs into her chest, and spoke sweetly to these bells. She asked if they were lonely and where they had all hung and what they thought of her father. She told them about her life in the way a child tells her grandparent a story of discovery.

After a few hours with the tower bells she walked, dust covered, in the same manner and sat beside the newer bells. She watched as the light bounced off their angles and smiled. She so wanted to caress their shiny, nubile bodies, but these bells made her bashful. She did not know them and they did not know her.

Before she left and locked the foundry she walked over and explored the equipment on the other side. There were strickle patterns in all different sizes, clay and loam to make the moulds, a runner box to move them, a furnace to melt the metal, a ladle and mould case to pour the liquid bells into shape, and a lathe to skirt and tune them. Emma ran her hand along and through each piece, remembering all the research she had done as she pressed her palms and fingers in and around the equipment. She lingered longer at the mould case, folding her body over the edge and staring down into its womb. There were cobwebs latticed on the inside and layers of shavings had settled along the walls and floor of the case. Emma sighed heavily; this cast was not meant to collect spiders and dust, it was meant to bear bells. Slowly she began sweeping her hands in large circles, collecting everything that stuck to the case walls, and flicking it outside onto the ground.

She wanted to make this world live again.

Before she slipped back outside and into the yard she turned to say goodbye to the bells that lived in the foundry. She promised them softly that she would be back and that they would never be lonely again.

With her mother and father wrapped in each other, she stole every evening away in the foundry. She sat on the floor beside the lathe with her notebook, sketched bells, and sang in tune. Emma knew that she wanted to create something beautiful. For a week she pressed pencil to paper and made curves, long and short, thick and thin, until she found the ones that struck her.

On the last boiling evening in July, the heat beat the sweat out of her and onto the page. Her hair stuck in strands against her cheek and she could smell the lead of her drawings. It was that night that Emma found the curve of her bell. Once drawn, her sticky fingers ran along the page so much it began to smudge. With leaded tips she stood up, held the sketch against her chest, and breathed it all inside her. Then, with sweat and proud elation, she began to make the strickle, pulling wood in and together to create the pattern of her curves.

August came and so did her moulding. She mixed the ingredients for loam, her father's bell making recipe, in a large copper kettle: clay, sand, horse hair, and village water. When it became thick and smooth, Emma picked up large clumps, slapped the dense mixture against her hands, and packed it into bricks. The loam and her sweat made her fingers stick together.

Once her bricks were finished, she used their rough outlines to begin the inner mould. Layer by layer, day by day, she'd push, sweat, and breathe deep breaths as the core of her bell began to take shape. Emma would build a layer, smooth it with hands, forearms, and body, and then measure it against the strickle to get the angles right. Once the core was built she set to work on the cope, the outer mould. She kneaded the loam into more precise curves for two weeks; her bell was budding. She shivered in the sticky evening heat as she worked; she could feel her excitement swirling in all the soft parts of her body.

When her mould was complete Emma could see the entire shape clearly. She longed to press her skin against it, embrace it, but it was still too weak to hold her weight. It was not yet a bell. She readied the runner box, made from steel rectangles and sand, and prepared for it to come to life. Emma pulled what she had made with pleasing exasperation, the sinews in her arms and legs stretched inside her as she and her creation made their way to the furnace.

Once the metals had melded together and stuck

inside her nostrils she put on her father's goggles and gripped the heavy ladle. She scooped the skin the metals had formed together on top of the cauldroned furnace off and onto the floor. It sat like volcanic ash and made the air move in waves. Then Emma carefully ladled the metals into her cast. With each laden scoop she could smell the casting. It was a very distinctive smell, one of earth and soot and sweat. It mixed with the August heat and made the air thick and heavy. The smell hung on her body and in her pores as she worked. She hoped it would hang there for days.

When she finished ladling the last of the metals into the cast Emma left the foundry. With her body covered in a wet mixture of shavings, dust, and sand, she let her teeth peek out the creases of her lips. Her bell was being born.

After two days of dreaming, Emma returned to the foundry to break her bell out and into the world. She quivered as she closed the heavy door behind her. The heat and smell still sat thickly along the walls and in the air. She clasped her hands around the rounded cups of her shoulders, tucked her head into their creases, and breathed a long fluttering breath. This was her moment, when the world became hers.

Emma approached the mould case with the same trepidation a man might approach his new lover's body. She was already dripping in the August heat. Slowly, she picked up the steel mallet that her father had used for so many years and felt the weight of it in her hands. She turned it, finding the grooves in each section of its wooden handle. Then, with one heavy breath and swing, Emma cracked the mallet into the mould to free her bell. The layers of loam she had smoothed for weeks fell away into piles of rubble and from beneath she could catch shapely glimpses of bronze. She swung the mallet feverishly against each side, and then dropped to her knees and began to peel away at its shell. When all the loam had fallen to the ground she sat on the floor, knees spread and hands outstretched, looking up at her bell.

She had created something beautiful.

As Emma stood to touch what had been born, her legs buckled; the excitement had stolen her energy. She stood quietly for a few moments, waiting to regain her strength before leading her bell to the lathe. Once the quivering in her legs had quieted, she closed her hands around the runner box, leaned low and heavy, and pressed her bell to its final destination. She unhooked the clasp of the lathe, brought it down onto the head of her bell, and used the weight and leverage to lift it off the box and into place. The edges of the bell were rough where the loam had crashed and broken away. Emma took the bit of the lathe and began running it and her hand delicately along the inner and outer curves of the bell. The shavings chipped and fell and stuck to her bare legs. The rough edges rounded, felt warm and smooth to touch, the curves were hipped and hour-glassed; the bell had grown into its body. And, when Emma stood by its side they made perfect ovals together.

Once her bell had taken shape, she had to let it sing. Emma sung the soft sweet notes— the prime, the octave, fifth, and minor third—as she lifted the tuning fork from the top corner of the lathe. She crouched down, smiling, and held the heavy fork along the lip of the bell. She swelled with anticipation as her hand touched the two together. Emma held her breath to hear it hum.

~

Christina Thatcher fell in love with Wales while studying for a Creative Writing MA at Cardiff University. Now as a postgraduate tutor and researcher, she is passionate about understanding how creative writing can improve the lives of vulnerable people. She has recently been published in *The London Magazine, Planet Magazine*, and the *Lampeter Review*, among others. Her website is at https://collectingwords.wordpress.com or follow her on Twitter @writetoempower.

Taking Shape, was inspired by a conversation with a fellow writer who mentioned that her friend owned the last operating bell foundry in London; Christina was instantly intrigued by this. She soon began researching bells and bell making and was surprised to find out that each part of the bell was named after a part of the body, which served to make her story more sensual than she originally envisioned it. Before starting the piece, Christina got in touch with a bell-maker's daughter and was so taken in by her world that she decided to make her main character the daughter of a bell maker as well. Since it is highly unlikely that Christina will ever become a bell maker herself, writing this story allowed her to indulge her curiosity and make it purposeful.

Woman in a White Room
Shelagh Middlehurst

It was another day like all the others. A cold blue sky above a grey grey world. No sun, no warmth. The woman was a slight figure lying on a narrow bed, eyes shut, arms by her sides; keeping still, keeping silent. Stuck behind her eyes was an image she could not erase. Sometimes it played in full blinding Technicolor, with reds so hot her eyeballs burned, with yellows so sharp they ripped her brain. And the black, so deep, so dark, a thick pitch that sucked her in, filling her nostrils, filling her mouth, stopping her breath. Today it played its relentless repeat in grainy black and white. An old movie not yet digitally re-mastered, the soundtrack crackly, the images ghostlike.

Beyond her eyelids was a room, white, bare, the door locked from the outside. One window to let in the day. This window never opened; high, barred, mesh covering the gaps so not even a fly could get in, or out.

She could hear footsteps from the world outside the room, heavy steps coming closer. The woman made a slight movement and her breathing quickened but her eyes stayed shut. The footsteps stopped. A key turned. The door opened quickly, quietly. A breath of different air from elsewhere – a whiff of cooking, an underlying aroma of cleaning fluid liberally used to mask the stench of bodily fluids – the cloying of blood, faeces, urine.

A person in a white coat approached the bed. The

101

woman kept her eyes shut, kept the reel running, kept the world out.

'How are you today?' the voice was professionally pleasant, a different voice from yesterday, a male voice. She could smell his soap; smell the crispness of his shirt, his polished shoes; the light slick of hair gel. Beneath the cage of her ribs her heart banged. The contents of her stomach – one cup of black coffee, one slice of white bread toasted, one dose of psychotropic drugs placed there reluctantly one hour before – shifted upwards. Her lower intestine twisted, pain caused her straightened legs to contract and her knees to bend. The spasm passed. The male person lowered her knees, speaking while he laid his stranger's hands on her; pressing her abdomen, asking about appetite, bowel movements, menstruation. The woman's silence filled the white room, echoing off the bare walls, reverberating in the empty space under the bed. She slipped further back inside herself.

The person, the man, the doctor, gave his head a shake, lips compressed. Behind a door in the corner of the room was a bathroom. He needed to wash his hands. He made his heavy way across the room, shoes squeaking on the vinyl floor. The woman suppressed an urge to scream. It had been so long since she'd heard her own voice. Did she have one? Had she ever had one? Maybe before. For a moment she considered before. It was getting harder. The world beyond, the world before, were growing fainter, fading into something like a dream, but not a dream. There must have been a time before. A time before this place, these people, these questions.

Hands washed and carefully dried, the man, the doctor, shut the bathroom door. One backward glance at the prone woman and he was gone. The persistent whirr of the extractor fan hummed behind the closed door. The noise, pointless, wasteful, began to fill her head. A cruel trick. Barefooted, she slipped into the bathroom trying not to disturb the air as she moved. She used the toilet then clicked the extractor into silence.

The bathroom was an inner space, its white-tiled walls windowless. It was never completely dark in her white world but in the semi darkness when she was aware of the night beyond, she would open her eyes. Then the images detached themselves from behind her eyes and played out along the white walls. A red dot, a pinprick, one tiny perfect sphere of blood would appear on the ceiling above her bed. She'd wait, breath trapped inside bursting lungs while the redness bloomed. Like blotting paper, the walls, the ceiling, would suffuse. Then drip. A metallic salty taste tainted her mouth, her lips felt warm and sticky.

The field would grow suddenly. Tall acid-yellow flowers enveloping the wall behind her bed, surrounding her, suffocating her with their pungent smell. She was in the earth. Black soil stopped her mouth, her hair crawled with tiny black wriggling things, ears stuffed deaf, open eyes staring at the violent yellowness. There was a sharpness. A pain. Inside her body the pain grew. Teeth gnawed deep in her centre. There was something shining in her hand. She plunged it again and again into the dark foulness on top of her.

Then there was something like sleep that wasn't sleep and waking that wasn't truly awake. And the faces of strangers looking and the voices of strangers asking. And the pain inside and the pain outside. Then she was inside the whiteness and the whiteness was not inside her.

~

Shelagh Middlehurst is married, a mother and grandmother and has lived in Cardiff for twenty-seven years.

Woman in a White Room was written after a flashback to an MS relapse but isn't only about that.

Other things crept in from somewhere inside Shelagh's head, from the place where imagination fuses with reality and the story writes itself.

Long Division
Carole Burns

It feels like one long night, the days that have passed since we arrived at this house where we used to spend so much time it almost felt like ours, and this dawn, after which we will leave again. Luminescent she looked that first night in the pale glow from the window: my wife, fresh from our walk to watch the moon rise over the Thérain. Her idea of course. She was always full of ideas. Even in that dim light I could see the beauty mark on her cheek. It darkened when she exercised, or talked animatedly with friends, or even just worked hard at her desk. Or was agitated.

"I'm sorry," I said. But the moment had slipped away. So many do.

We'd been here only a few minutes when we decided to take a walk before the light disappeared altogether. We put on the Wellies left by the English couple who owned the house, and headed across the field toward the woods and stream where once we had walked in a rainstorm in these same borrowed boots. We sloshed into the brook to the other side and meandered through the small village of Canny-sur-Thérain. The houses were lit orange from inside as if the French still used candles at night. An occasional phrase floated through the early spring air, "*Merveilleux!*" "*Mon cher*" and then, as we passed the smell of cooking, "*Ce canard est très bon.*" We laughed. "Why do I feel at home here?" Rae mused, and I reached for her hand, cool in the air of the approaching night. We have lived in Cardiff now for a decade, the University accommodating both my mathematics and her linguistics (*math with words*, she used to call it), but sometimes we still felt a separation between ourselves and that land, between ourselves and the voices, though we couldn't quantify it. We never felt the same distance here.

I was comforted too by the solidness of her short body as she walked beside me. She is slender but squared off somehow – like a long division symbol, her sparkiness in that initial, upward check that connects to the long bar over the dividend. I am tall and lanky like a quaver, and I worry sometimes that she can't reach me. That she stops before I begin.

We walked for a while, then circled back in the dark, later than we should have without a torch, though the moon was bright enough, casting shadows in our path – the bushes in the dirt road between the houses, the wall of the house of the *très bon* duck, the trees slanting tall and thin toward the stream as if directing our route. Our presence in this spot of the earth is so precise, so unlikely when measured against the vastness of possibilities of people and places on the globe: Rae and I at Canny-sur-Thérain. Latitude, 49.601 degrees North; longitude, 1.72 degrees East. Two of us on one pinpoint.

"How does this happen?" I asked, calculating the possibilities. "One with one. On one."

"Equals one," she said.

This was an old debate, she always sticking up for the idea of two merging into one couple (word singular); I, the mathematician, seeing two separate whole integers even when joined into one set.

"Equals two," I corrected her, easily, as I used to.

She stopped walking. "Equals three."

I said nothing.

"Sometimes," she added quietly.

The night became silent then, as if the owls, the wind, the Frenchmen in their glowing houses, were embarrassed by our argument. We resumed walking. Then, past the last house, "*Où est ma petite fille?*" *Where is my little girl?*

We arrived back and Rae stood inside in the moonlight taking off her scarf, her coat, her face turned away from me until I said I was sorry. She glared purposefully at the floor.

I had not wished to try. I had calculated the odds and for us in particular they were slim indeed. "I hate your numbers!" she'd cried out once. But I did not see how the hours of planning and minutes of effort could outweigh the heft of those figures, how the blossoming of hope would not drown us both as it turned into grief. I may have been wrong but my calculations were right. "Once," she had pleaded, "at least once," and it was here in the dusk of a warm summer day when we learned it hadn't worked; we had not been back since.

Are we not complete in ourselves? I wanted to ask. Each set is complete, each subset itself a set, complete on its own. Could we be made incomplete by something that does not yet, might not ever, exist?

She stood still and silent and firm.

"I know you're sorry," she finally said. "I know you're sorry we weren't able to – did not – have a child." She nodded vigorously as if convincing herself all over again. "But you're not sorry. About our decisions."

She took a breath and held it in – her body

suspended in it. I was suspended in it, too. A window creaked. An owl hooted. She waited for me to disagree. I did not. She breathed out. Switched on a lamp. Made tea.

Now after three days of walking around each other as well as the land I stand alone watching the sunrise.

So many moments lost. Even those lost in this house could barely be counted up, each four-day weekend containing so many of them. We'd been here maybe five or six weekends every year, and we've been coming here now for nine years, though we stayed only twice the first year we discovered the house, so that would be 5.1 with 1 as a repeating decimal weekends per year that we've been here. I multiply that by hours of daylight and a few moonlit hours when we've both been awake, and add the three weeklong holidays we'd had as well, which means if there were even one lost moment in each hour together that alone was one thousand seventy-one, point 9, repeating decimal, lost moments. Which is nothing compared to the moments lost in an entire lifetime, so numerous we couldn't possibly remember them all let alone realize they were beyond our reach. They were all lost, the moments; even those that had been grasped were gone now.

"Dah-vid." My name said the Welsh way.

Rae was standing at the doorway, her red robe flaring under her black hair, lengthening her petite figure.

"You're counting," she says.

I turn back toward the window to gaze at the weak rays of the sun rising over the Thérain. I cannot help but look at the sun directly although she always tells me not to. "There's so much to take away," I say.

Then she's in front of me, blocking the light, holding both my hands, her beauty mark milky black in the dawn. "Count for me," she says. And I do.

~

Carole Burns's collection, *The Missing Woman and Other Stories*, is published by Parthian Books. She is a reviewer for the Washington Post and editor of *Off the Page: Writers Talk About Beginnings, Endings, and Everything in Between*, a book based on interviews with 43 writers, including Andrea Levy, Colm Tóibín and A.S. Byatt. She is Head of Creative Writing at the University of Southampton and lives in Cardiff.

Long Division came out of her project, "Imagistic," which invites writers to respond to images from particular artists with pieces of flash fiction. 'It was the place in a painting by Tig Sutton that inspired this piece – a small village in Normandy. I've visited Tig there, and have taken the walk that these characters take. The idea of past times being present when we revisit a place animated this story as well.'

The two Sutton paintings to which this story responds – 'Moonrise Over the Thérain Valley' and 'The Sun Rises Over the Thérain River' – can be viewed on her Website: www.caroleburns.com

His Shoes
Barrie Llewelyn

There were shoes by the back door when I came in with the shopping. Big as boats shaped like black and yellow bananas. Automatically, I bent over to put them away. There's an Ikea trunk for shoes beneath the stairs. For our shoes: Charlotte's school shoes; her flip-flops and trainers; my slip-ons and work-shoes and wellies for the garden. I was going to pick up these rogue, foreign shoes, left carelessly so that someone might trip over them and put them with the others. Then I stopped. These were aliens, not mine to touch or move. It's been a long time since there were man things in this house. I left them where they were. But then, at the last minute, turned them so that they were on their way out, ready to leave.

I turned away too and shouted towards the living room, 'I'm back,' and as I made my way to the kitchen, I thought again about yesterday and the day before and the weeks before that when we were still on C1. So many days and nights and every twenty-four hours another dose of *the beast*. The doctors called it ALG and tried to explain what it was and how it would help us but they glossed over what it would do to Charlotte every time it was fed into her through her Hickman. *We have to make you ill, to make you better*. How many times did I hear that apology and watch Charlotte nod her acceptance through rigours and cold sweats and rash? We dealt with it in the way we've always dealt with everything: as they wheeled the metal pole in and connected the IV to it and to her, I

110

only had to look at Charlotte and we'd mouth the word *beast* to each other at the same time. We'd giggle and try to hold that moment as long as we could, tried not to think of how long it would be this time before the side effects – which had no other side but nasty – began.

'I'm back,' I said again as I walked through to the living room. 'And I've thought if I use Milton to sterilise the lettuce you can have your Caesar salad, I even got you a tin of anchovies – I thought we could take a walk to the shop and get a film out for late...'

The room was empty. I'd left her propped on pillows and surrounded by juice and magazines only half an hour before.

'Hey. I'm back,' I called up the stairs.

'Great. Be down now. Hope you've got food,' Charlotte called from her room.

A minute or two later, she was down the stairs and in the kitchen, the boy was just behind her. The owner of the banana boat trainers. Both of them were going through my Tesco bags.

'Mum, James wants to eat with us, okay?'

'Sure,' I said, 'Hi James, have we met?'

Charlotte giggled and rolled her eyes in exasperation with me. 'Every day in hospital, Mum, James was there.'

I hadn't noticed.

Charlotte's room in the bone marrow transplant unit was purple. Late in the mornings Penny came in to clean the purple room. She had a special mop in a bucket marked 'purple' and with it she moved bits of dirt and hair and sometimes dried blood from place to place. She mopped last, moving herself out of the room, telling us stories about her grand-daughter:

about your age and just as pretty, duck. Penny was working to pay for her granddaughter's tuition to a boarding school for dancers in Leeds or Loughborough. I could never remember which and didn't like to keep asking. Before she mopped, she'd shuffle the get well cards along the windowsill from place to place so that she could wipe over the surface, commenting all the time on the amount of cards there were and the gifts and all the visitors in and out. *How popular you are, duck.* And Charlotte, no doubt about it, glowed at the attention of this quick little woman, while I sat in my corner chair, lifting my legs up for the mop to slide under. And every time it did, my heart filled with the endlessness of time in that purple room.

There aren't visiting hours in the unit. People have to scrub up and put on a gown, but as long as you aren't actually recovering from a transplant, anyone can wander in to see you any time of day. I scrubbed and gowned, but of course I wasn't a visitor, I was there to be with Charlotte: to get her food if she was hungry; to stand outside the cubicle while she showered; to dry her hair; paint her nails; wheel her to x-ray, watch for signs of distress when they attached her to the beast. Run out into the corridor to get help.

I spent the nights on that cold leather chair in the corner of the room under the lamp and the call button. The chair was ripped and grubby with dirt in corners, which was a little incongruous with the sterile gown I was required to keep on while I tried to sleep. A kind nurse gave me a blanket and I put it over that chair rather than myself. Still I couldn't help thinking of those other mothers that had sat there before me just as terrified at two, three, four o'clock in the morning listening not to hospital noises – nurses' tea-cups or the temperature and blood pressure trolley making its rounds – but to the evenness of their child's sleeping breath.

Some nights when she asked me to and when I wouldn't be in the way of her tubes, in and out, I climbed into the bed and stayed till the hospital radio played Dancing Queen at six am to wake everyone up. Those were the best times, when I could hold my beautiful girl, touch her silky hair. Then it was like it had always been, just her and me; no one to interrupt while I looked after her.

In the morning, evening and the middle of the day there were visitors: boys and girls Charlotte knew from school, from various part-time jobs, from nights out. I recognised some of her oldest friends, of course, but I was surprised at how so many youngsters who I didn't know came to see her. I could see Charlotte change when her friends were there. Her colour came back; it was good to hear her laugh. The purple room became a common room in school or a café in the centre of Cardiff and as the room became busier the nurses lingered after their checks, drawn in by the sound of teenagers.

After a while I'd leave them. The coffee shop was also the staff canteen and there were two prices for everything. I drank tea at the higher price and looked straight at the overhead TV. It was usually Wimbledon or highlights from Wimbledon, but it might have been an earthquake killing off the population of Mid Wales and I wouldn't have noticed. I never saw any of it. I was just waiting a reasonable time until I could go back to her. Visitors are a good thing, but they shouldn't stay too long. Charlotte was undergoing treatment, she needed to rest. I needed to make sure Charlotte got some rest.

I should have noticed James. The day after that first supper, she told me about him. He'd visited her every day in hospital, most days twice. How had I missed him? Just before she became ill, he began to drive her home from school. Why hadn't I known about it? He lived nearby, she said. She'd known him for a long time, as you know local boys, faces in school. They were just friends, she said.

Just friends. That was supposed to make me feel better about the time he spent with her upstairs in her room. I knew they were lying in her bed together. Most nights he didn't leave until very late, well after Charlotte had fallen asleep. I tried to get used to the bed thing, after all Charlotte was supposed to be resting between daily visits to the out-patient unit for her continuing treatment. I told myself that if they were just friends, this was okay. Still, after a week or so, I couldn't help but mention it.

'We're only watching TV or listening to music,' Charlotte said in a way that told me there was no point saying anything else about it.

I couldn't help but hear her laughter and his rolling voice, the way he was in the house. The way he came in and threw off his shoes, stretched himself out on the settee for a few minutes, even making small talk with me, before they went upstairs. The way he made regular trips to the kitchen to check out the contents of the fridge, make sandwiches. The way he fed her and brought her things. Like my time in that purple room – very soon James was no longer a visitor.

Still, the days with her were mine. James had to go to school, and we had our trips to the day unit together. It was a place for the shuffling elderly, for chemo infiltrations and blood transfusions. For Charlotte, it was a place of waiting and being restless, of realising how an illness can shrink your world to the next pill, the next temperature check, the next needle, scan, blood count. I tried to make it better. I bought *Heat* and *Hello* and on good days we studied those magazines and commented on what Victoria Beckham was wearing or why anyone would want to take so many pictures of her. On those days, I could make her laugh in the way we had together, making faces at one of the bossy nurses or talking to her in a silly whisper trying not to be heard, trying to keep everything between us.

There were other times though. And I couldn't help but notice that as the weeks wore on they became more frequent. Charlotte would be uncommunicative; she'd walk into the unit with her earphones on, the volume of her iPod all the way up. She'd pretend not to hear anything the receptionist, or the nurses, or I said to her. She'd pull faces and turn away if another patient acknowledged her with a smile or tried to speak, leaving me to make polite conversations I wasn't in the mood for either. And then when the frustration finally boiled up, it was me that she'd turn on. It was sudden.

'You don't have to be here, you could go back to work, you can go shopping. I have to be here but you don't,' she said one day, the poison from the beast in her voice.

'Charlotte, sweetheart. I don't want to be anywhere else. I want to be with you.'

'I don't need you with me. I know the routine.'

'Don't be like this with me,' I pleaded as quietly as I could. There were other patients close by. There were nurses, social workers, a receptionist. It was afternoon; everyone seemed paralysed around us, connected to a machine. Everyone wanted something interesting to happen. I didn't want us to entertain them and I didn't want anyone else to know that Charlotte wasn't just a sweet, sick teenager and I, her ever-doting mother. I didn't want to admit what the drugs were doing to her; what being ill was doing to her. And even more than that, I knew that some of this was about James. She would much rather he was there than me. That was the thought that brought the tears to my eyes. It was the worst thing I could do. She saw the tears and I have never seen her harden so.

'It's not your disease. Why are you crying?'

She said it out loud and clearly. I felt the pores open on my back and under my arms. I felt my healthy blood pound through my body, like it's supposed to. I should have been more like a mother is supposed to be. I should not have fled from the day unit. I should have smiled and laughed it off; brought out some Haribo candy, produced a new magazine for us to laugh over. I should have done all those things because an hour later, I had to return and face everything I had not done. Quietly admit to everything I was incapable of being for her. I had to act like everything was normal when my daughter looked through me and then ignored me all the way home.

His shoes are by the back door. Charlotte and James are in the living room watching the Simpsons. I can hear her low conforming laughter – even I remember how you change things about yourself when you are falling in love.

I've been shopping. I've brought them food. Coke

and crisps and our dinner. James doesn't like fish or carrots. So maybe, by not having those things on the menu, I can tempt him to stay. Sometimes he goes home and eats with his parents, but he always comes back half an hour later and anyway I need him here more than they need him at home.

I can't help going into the room to see them. I feel her head for temperature and though she hasn't spoken to me for most of the day, because he is here, she lets me touch her.

'There's pizza for dinner,' I say and they both nod and Charlotte smiles at me like she always has.

Before I do anything else – water the garden, pay bills, put the pizzas in the oven, I need to get his shoes out of the way. He's always leaving them where someone could trip over them.

It's late – past midnight and there is no more noise coming from her room. No music or the muffled sounds of their talk and their laughter. I think they have fallen asleep. I wonder vaguely if James has an overnight bag or a toothbrush and then I think maybe I have dozed off and he has gone home. When I think this, I feel my heart stop.

But downstairs, his shoes are in the place where I left them. I pick them up and hold them for a while. They're so big – and yet how big can they really be? I think maybe I should clean them, as far as I know he wears them every day; they deserve to be cared for. In the kitchen I lie them on paper towels and spread the laces out of the way. With Fairy on a J-cloth, I begin to wipe them down, working from back to front. The leather is hardly cracked; I think of how James is gentle, easy on his things. With an old toothbrush, I clean the grooves on the soles. They are surprisingly clean anyway. James is careful where he steps, I think. I start to cry.

I hold his shoes close to my dressing gown and take them into the living room. I open the curtains a bit and see where they have left empty Coke cans and half a bowl of smelly crisps on the coffee table. Preferring the dark, I close the curtains again and sit where they sat earlier, before they'd gone to bed. I begin to rock.

Back and forth, I hold his shoes and rock. I must have stopped crying because now I am humming a love song and floating. Back and forth with his shoes, I am somewhere else.

After a while, in the kitchen, I stuff his shoes with more kitchen roll. It will help them keep their shape and I tie the laces. It takes me four attempts, but finally the bows are equal to each other and perfect.

And then I put them away for the rest of the night. Not in our trunk, but near it. Very close.

~

Barrie Llewelyn is a writer and editor. She teaches Creative Writing to undergraduates and supervises MPhil and PhD students at the University of South Wales.

'This story, **His Shoes**, was written shortly after my 16 year old daughter spent time in hospital being treated for Aplastic Anaemia. When I workshopped the story at Ty Newydd, another writer cried as I read it which I thought was a good result. But one of the tutors told me that I could never publish it because it was too personal. Though, it didn't take long for me to let it go; that crazed, shoe-loving mother is not me! Not at all!'

Lick
Kate North

It started growing the morning after his 30th birthday. Paul woke with a hangover and as he lay in bed, staring at the ceiling, he felt a little lump on his palm. He didn't worry about it. It's not a place one gets worried about. If it had been on his neck or his groin then he would have gone to the doctor's straight away.

It became solid gradually. It had started out like a blister, a ball of fluid skinned over. Then it firmed up becoming the size of a small thimble. It was slightly darker than the rest of the skin on his palm. After a while it became a deeper pink and then it widened out like a fat leaf. Eventually he was able to flap it from one side of his palm to the other.

He wasn't a hairy man. When it started to sprout tiny little hairs, and there were still no answers to be found on Google, he booked a doctor's appointment. It wasn't for two weeks though. He couldn't bring himself to say he needed one sooner. The receptionist was really nosey. She would ask personal questions in a loud voice when the waiting room was busy. 'Is it urgent Mr Bevan, or can it wait?'

He had become adept at disguising it by now. He was right handed and so had learned to offer his left hand when greeting people. He even managed to get into writing with his left hand. When he went out socially he kept his right hand tucked in his jeans' pocket as much as possible. Also, because the growth was flattish, it lay along his palm like one of those fortune telling fish you get from Christmas crackers. It didn't stick out at an angle or anything. That's how he had been able to put up with it for so long.

He had a date later in the week. He met Gemma a few months back on his lunch break. She worked in the same building for a different company. They had both been having their lunch in the quad. They were on opposite benches eating out of noodle boxes from the Thai place by the station. He had been checking his phone when he looked up and saw her. She smiled at him and he smiled back. The next time he saw her, a week later, she was eating a falafel wrap from the Turkish place near the cinema and so was he. He asked her out and she said yes.

They were meeting for drinks at half past seven. If it was horrific they could go their separate ways after one or two. If it was great they could go for something to eat. He was a little worried about the growth. He didn't want her to see it, obviously. If they ended up going for food he would have to be careful. If they went for Italian he could choose pasta and eat it with a fork in his left hand. Little pasta bows or twirls would be perfect. Of if they went for Chinese he could have noodles.

He walked into the bar and scanned the room for her. She wasn't there yet so he got a drink and sat at a table by a window. It had become his habit to flick the growth back and forth with his fingers. It could get quite sweaty as it was the summer and he worried that it might start to smell. It reminded him of a picture he had seen in a biology textbook during high school. It was of a girl with a 'tropical disease'. One side of her head looked completely normal but the other side was all puffed up like a blowfish. Just above her eyebrow a fold of skin pulled down across her face making her look like she had had a stroke. The picture was so grotesque everyone turned to it when the textbooks were handed out. Most copies actually fell open to that particular page, anticipating the curious faces that would peer over the picture uttering 'grooooooooss,' and 'uuuuuuugly'. Paul imagined a picture of his own hand in a biology textbook, a cluster of young heads bent over it in shock and disgust. He wondered if he would be paid royalties for such an image.

He saw Gemma arrive through the door and shocked himself by digging his nails into the growth. He was nervous and it wasn't like him. She looked gorgeous. She was wearing a blue polka dot dress and a massive white sunhat that would have looked ridiculous on anyone else. She took the hat off and fanned her face with it while she looked across the bar. He liked the way she puffed air out of her cheeks making her fringe flutter. He raised his left hand and waved, sliding his right hand into his back pocket. She smiled and headed over. They did cheek kisses and he offered to get her a drink. 'No, no, it's okay,' she said and strode off to the bar. She came back to the table with a glass that had two straws, a slice of orange, a cocktail stirrer and a little paper umbrella in it.

Conversation was easy. They spoke and spoke and spoke. They were close in age and had been to similar schools on opposite sides of town. They had both done ology degrees. She had taken sociology and he had taken psychology. He bought a round of drinks and this time hers came with two slices of orange. She prodded them to the bottom of the glass and smiled at him, 'Fruit soaks up alcohol,' she said. She worked as an analyst for a company with a really long name so they used an acronym. He told her about being a team leader for Barnett & Barrett and about how he didn't mind it but that he was looking for something else. He wasn't really sure what though. They even had some mutual acquaintances, it turned out. A friend of a friend and one of her second cousins also.

When she got to the bottom of her drink she fished the slices of orange out with the cocktail stirrer. She placed them both on her hand and proffered them to him, 'Want one?' she asked. He took a slice with his left hand, and following Gemma's lead, he put it to his mouth and bit into the flesh. It tasted of the cocktail and juice spilled down his chin. She chuckled and dabbed his face with a serviette then wiped her hands with it. They sat smiling in silence for a moment and it wasn't at all awkward. Then he said, 'Did you know that inside of that cocktail umbrella, there are tightly wound rolls of Chinese newspaper wrapped around the tiny little pole?'

'Paul Bevan, I did not know that,' she said in mock disbelief as she raised an eyebrow. 'Show me,' she then said pushing her glass towards him. He would need two hands to do this but it was okay. He could do it without showing her the growth. He took the umbrella in his right hand, his palm facing him and the back of his hand facing her. Then, with his left hand he picked at the paper at the top of the pole then pulled it away. It streamed out like bunting and caused the little umbrella to spin in his right hand. It was like a child's magic trick. Gemma smiled and grabbed the thin strip of Chinese newspaper from him. She spread it out on the table between them, 'I wonder what it says?' she asked. 'You are in luck,' said

Paul, 'I am fluent in Cantonese.' Her pupils widened, 'No?' she said. Paul bent forward and considered the newspaper in front of him. 'It says, two spring rolls, satay chicken skewers, beef in black bean sauce and rice or noodles, £9.99 all in.' Gemma burst out laughing, 'I can't believe I fell for that.' 'Do you fancy it though? A Chinese?'

She did fancy a Chinese and went off to powder her nose before they left. He really liked her. She was clever, and funny and very attractive. She liked his jokes and he was relaxed in her company. There had even been that silent moment.

At Lin's they ordered a set meal for two and they took their time between courses. They drank big bottles of Chinese beer and they talked about countries they had travelled to and places they would like to visit. They both disliked people who had been to India and 'found themselves' and they shared an interest in going to cold places like Scandinavia and Iceland. By the time they had finished their meal it was obvious that they would be seeing each other again. He wondered what to suggest. He didn't want to be too full on but he did hope that she would invite him back to hers.

Walking towards her house they discussed their favourite parts of the city. She liked the castle at night. The way it sat all square and dark and solid, right in the centre of town. She also liked the lake, particularly in winter when it was iced over like a mirror. He liked City Road because you could eat something from almost every country in the world since there were so many restaurants. He also liked the stadium because it reminded him of watching matches with his dad, and of coming second in the county cup when he was 14 and because when it was a match day you could hear the singing and the chanting carried across the city with the breeze even if you were a mile or two away.

The nearer they got to her house the slower they walked. Her street was particularly long and as they came to the beginning of it a small hedgehog was making its way across the road. 'Awwwhh, look,' she said, pointing it out, 'a little hedgehog, it's sooooo cute.' They walked over to it. Paul was feeling a little tipsy and he supposed that Gemma was too. The hedgehog froze as they loomed above it. Gemma bent down to pick it up and its spikes fanned out in defence. 'I think we might be freaking it out,' said Paul. She stood back up and sighed. Then she grabbed his right arm and swung it across her shoulders. He pulled away instinctively then relaxed as he realised the growth was not in her line of sight. He hoped that she hadn't noticed his jolt of unease. They made their way towards her house with his arm draped around her. They discussed where they would go next time. He wanted to try a new Turkish place and she was up for it. The sky was dark and there were few stars visible though they could make out a satellite and a plane that had taken off from the airport. They wondered where the plane was heading, maybe Iceland or Scandinavia but more likely Malaga or Paris.

As they got to the front of her house she leaned into him, her nose against his shoulder, and took a deep breath. He couldn't tell if he was about to be invited in or not. He leaned down and kissed the top of her head. She looked up at him as he said, 'I've had an amazing night.' She moved towards him and they kissed for what felt like minutes. Her lips were soft and slightly sweet from the pineapple ice cream they had shared at the end of the meal. She placed both her hands around his neck and they kissed again. He became lost in her kiss and her sweet, fruity smell and the darkness of the evening. Then she leaned back and trickled her hands down each of his arms coming to a stop when they were stood hand in hand, observing each other as mirror images.

Then she squealed and pulled away, raising her left hand to her face. 'What was that?' she said. She stepped back examining her hand and he could see the upstairs curtains moving in the house next-door. 'Shhh,' he said, 'it's okay.' He cupped his right hand in the palm of his left, it was fisted into a ball, hiding the growth. 'I felt something,' she said, 'it was like a dog licking me, what was it?' She looked up at him, her eyes wide. 'I don't know,' he said, and his eyes moistened but didn't form tears. She grabbed his hand and he didn't resist. She pulled at his fingers until his fist opened like a flower in which she could see the tongue-like growth flopping from side to side across his palm.

~

Kate North is the author of *Bistro* (2012), a poetry collection and *Eva Shell* (2008), a novel. She is interested in urban life and the impact of technology on writing and identity. She is also interested in communicating scientific and medical subjects through creative writing.

www.katenorth.co.uk

Of 'Lick' she says, 'I was trying to write about the unexpected arriving in the everyday, particularly from an urban perspective. Most people live in towns and cities and most people have banal daily routines that just chug along until something unexpected happens. I wanted to write about how these unexpected occurrences can help to form or fracture relationships, how they can change the trajectory of people's lives.'

Letters Home
Susmita Bhattacharya

2nd January 2005

My dear Asma,

Salaam-alekum. I reach Cardiff all safe and sound, and start working also. The plane journey so terrible. Seat so tiny and they not show nice Hindi film. Old flop film. No Amitabh Bachchan no Shah Rukh Khan. I waste my money on this plane. Nizambhai go last year in British Airways, and see latest film, *Ab Tak Chappan*. Remember we see this in Paradise Talkies, just after marriage? Food was so-so. Cold rice and dal. Hard hard chana masala. Chicken like cricket ball.

I am in Cardiff now. Very fine city. By bus three hours from Heathrow. Sorry, by coach. Bus, coach all same things. When you come to UK you also learn many new English words like me. So I practise to write English with you every letter, okay? You reading loud and practise talking loud. We pass English exam fast and we get British citizenship fast. Muyazzumbhai waiting for me at bus-stop. Here bus-stop is so big and not crowded. I do not have to push to get into bus or out. Everyone stand in line. In queue. But one thing not good about Cardiff. I find out soon. It is raining raining all the time. Small small drops, like mist. Not like in Dhaka, big fat rain that fall like stones. And so cold, I cannot say how much. My bones feel like *kulfi*. I think I am inside a fridge. So freezing and misty and dark. Muyazzambhai bring for me a big, black coat. It is very warm. Once I'm inside this coat, I like Cardiff once again!

I am sharing big house with three men. 2 Bengalis and one from Syria. We all work in Muyazzumbhai's restaurant. Is very big and famous restaurant fifteen minutes' walk from house. Royal Bengal Cuisine. But there is no Bengali food. Something called curry. Nothing like home food. All food here called curry this and curry that. I so confused. I learning to make chicken tikka masala and doner kebabs. But I assistant, so I not cooking food in restaurant. Just cutting and chopping now. I cooking at home only. Abdulmia says I making better kebabs than head chef. But that is secret, as we not wanting to lose job. I go to English school in the morning. Very nice school. People from all countries. One Bengali lady in my class, but she very British. She not talking to me. My teacher, her name is Betty. Her hair more golden than your bangles.

How are you? Hope all is fine at home. Ammi is good to you? You taking care of yourself. Soon you come here when baby is born.

I write again soon,

Hassan.

My name is Hassan Sadikur. I come from Bangladesh. I live in Cardiff. I am married. What about you?

10th February 2005

Dear Wife,

I got your letter. But rain falling on it and I cannot read very well. Next time write with ball point pen, not pencil. Happy New Year to you. Don't worry, Betty teacher is old. She married and has big son. She not pretty like you, but her hair is golden.

Our house very beautiful. In UK, it is called terraced house. Many many many houses stand in one line. Long queue. All looking same. One night I coming home and not finding my house. I standing on the road and looking. All same – same colour, same curtains, same doors. I getting very scared. I lost in this new country, this long street with same houses. I don't know anyone to ask. I ask one lady in the street. But she scared more than me. She say something I not understanding and she run inside one house. She close the door bang in front of me. In my area, most people not speak English. I think so. More Bengali. But this lady – what she speak, I not understand.

Then I remember, all houses have a number. This door with scared lady inside has 29 on it. My door is 119. My house in UK. Muyazzumbhai says it is 5101 miles away from Dhaka. But everyday I smell Bangladeshi cooking smell coming from next house and I close my eyes. Then Dhaka is very close by...

My wife's name is Asma Begum. She is 20 years old. She has long, black hair and black eyes. She wears pink sari and pink scarf. She cries because I go away to UK.

19th February 2005
Dear Asma,

Today strange thing happened. I was walking down street when I see footpath green in colour. I look close by and see small small small pieces of glass. Full street covered. I stand and look. So pretty they look. Shining in the sun. Yesterday Wales winning rugby match against France. People going mad. I can see stadium from my house. Big stadium with big arms sticking out in the sky, like monster spider. I hear shouts and singing from inside. Like how we can hear shouting from Dhanmondi Stadium when cricket match is on. I remember sitting outside stadium with transistor and cigarettes, shouting with the crowd inside. Here people celebrating with beer all night. And they breaking bottles on the road, I don't know why. Maybe celebration tradition like that. I don't know how to play rugby, so I ask man from Somalia who sit next to me in class. He not knowing also and he live in UK four years. He saying it is all fighting on the field. So I watch on TV highlights and get headache. Too much *dishum-dishum*, little bit playing. I not understanding. Here no cricket on TV or on radio. Muyazzumbhai call Bangladesh every ten minutes to know score. He having too much money to spend.

Do you watch cricket match with Abba and Ammi? When I go home next time, we will go to stadium and see live cricket, okay?

Hassan

Would you like to give the order, sir? What would you like to drink? Mineral water, fizzy or still? Anything else? Thank you, sir, will that be all? Do come again, good-night.

5th March 2005
Dear Asma

How are you? Why you getting headache? What the doctor said? Is everything okay? You take care of baby inside you, okay? No feel sad. I tell you a new story now. Maybe you smile.

Customers in Royal B.C. like the food. Yesterday Rafiqmia made mistake and gave too hot too spicy food to *gora* man yesterday. His face turning red like beetroot and he cough coughing. He saying bad words to waiter from Syria, his name Ivan and throw curry on the floor. His friend laughing all the time. They both shouting loud and banging on table. They say they complain and close down restaurant. Muyazzumbhai gave free dinner to them, but when they go out, they wink and show finger and run. I not understanding these people. They go to pub and drink. Then they come for curry again, but man with beetroot face vomit on table. Muyazzumbhai call police. They run away and now we have to give policemen free curry. Take-away.

I have. You have. He has. She has. It has. They have. We have. I haven't. You haven't. He hasn't. They haven't. We haven't.

25th March 2005
Dear Asma,

I am so happy today. God is good to us. You take care of yourself. You haven't written to me. I'll pray for a healthy baby. You must not do too much work. No heavy-duty work. Sleep in the afternoon. Next month, I'll ask Ammi to send you to your Ammi's house, okay? I'll send you money soon.

I had first exam today. Speaking and listening. One teacher came from London, and she asked me questions. I can say all the answers, very easy like. Then I have to ask her questions. Her name is Sian. I say it is man's name in Bangladesh. I ask her to spell, but it is something else only. S-I-A-N. Shaan. I think nice name for boy, innit? But no good. When you come to Cardiff, people will laugh and say you give boy a girl's name. I asked her if she is married. She said no, she isn't. Then I make big mistake. I ask her if she has children. I bite my tongue. I'm sure I fail now. She says yes, a boy. I bite my tongue again. She's not good lady. But man from Somalia say many women here not married and have children, He know this because he been here 4 years. When you come here, you not speak to such ladies. Then Betty-teacher say she has partner, not husband and I'm sad. She's such a nice lady. I tell her you have baby soon, *insha-allah*. Betty teacher very happy for me and she say, congratulations. Like when passing exams. I am very happy and proud man today. My Asma having baby soon.

Love

Hassan

Baby –
babieslady-ladiesman-menwoman-womenchild-
children

9th May 2005

Dear Lovely Wife,

I am happy you are in your mother's house. Take rest there. Tell your Ammi to make chicken soup for you. Very good. I will try and send you chicken soup from here. Rafiqmia is going to Bangladesh. I will send you Baxter's soup. I will buy from Tesco. You know, from supermarket, very very big shop. Maybe big like football stadium. When I go there, I am nervous. So many things I see, I forget what to buy. When I think of Rehana stores in Dhaka, I laugh. It is smaller than one aisle in Tesco. And Tesco not just one supermarket. Sainsbury, Asda, Lidl, ... more, more, more. My head go round and round when I see so many things. So much food. From where they come? From Kenya, Argentina, Spain, from far far away. I want to eat *muri*, but cannot find in any of these supermarkets. I go to tiny Bangladeshi shop in Clare Road, and there I find my food. *Muri, daal, ilish maach* – frozen of course. But I hear you cannot eat fish anymore. Not liking smell? So now I will not eat *ilish maach* also. It is cheaper here than at home.

I buy some baby clothes. I know you will say bad luck to buy before baby comes, but what to do? Now special price, buy one get one free. I also buy, no, bought nappies. Pampers. Don't get angry. I will keep in Champa-*khala's* house if you want. Please send me photo of what you are looking like now. Champa-*khala's* daughter-in-law having baby also. And her son have photo of baby inside stomach. I cannot believe it. Then he showed me, and I think, this like E.T., that *bhoot* in the film. He get very angry. What to do, better not to see what you not supposed to see. I only see my baby when he coming out, not like *bhoot* inside tummy.

Write soon

Hassan

I'm sorry but I have a bit of a problem… I've afraid that… Please could I have my money back? … If you don't mind… Please can I exchange this for a larger size? …

1st June 2005

Dearest,

It was raining today and I ~~go~~ went inside a bus-stop. Here bus-stop has roof and bench to sit on. And bus come and go like trains in Dhaka – with a timetable. Many people sitting inside. All talking about rain. How hard is raining. They saying 'tipping it'. I look at sky and suddenly I laugh. I laugh and laugh, and people scared of me. They move far away. But I look at the rain and think, in Bangladesh when the roofs fly, we complain about the rain. Here umbrella fly and people are worried.

But it is good here. At least umbrella fly. Big umbrella cost £2.99. There roof fly, cannot buy new roof. No money. But don't worry, I send money to Abbajan for repair on roof. No more plastic sheet on top of kitchen roof.

I watch on TV, floods in England. Very bad situation. But everything so good, every person is getting bottled water from government and helicopter come to save people and their cats and dogs. I say what a great country. In Bangladesh, when floods come, we drink cholera water and pick up dead babies from water with our hands. What a lucky country this... our son must grow up here. You will come here soon.

Hassan

Mustafa is Somali. Asif is Pakistani. Maria is Polish. Hassan is Bangladeshi. Abdullah is Afghani. Li Jian is Korean. Nao is Japanese. Ahmed is Iraqi. Bahaar is Kurdish... the bombers are Muslim.

20th July, 2005
Dear Asma,

The bombers were Mussalman. Just like that. What is their country? Doesn't matter. What is their language? Doesn't matter. They are Muslim – that matters. I know now all Muslims can be terrorists. I'm afraid to go out. *I'm sorry I have a bit of a problem –* I'm Muslim. The terrorists bombed the station in London on July 7th. And you know what? Muyazzum-bhai was in London that day. And you know what? He never come back. He was the bomber? Or the victim? How do we know, because he is Muslim? What do we tell his wife and sons? Will his sons, so sweet young boys become terrorists to revenge for their father? Now I walk the long street in shame. I'm not ever looking up. Some boys here, shout Bin Laden when I pass by. They spit and laugh and run. I want to cry. Bin Laden kill my Muyazzumbhai. Do I look like terrorist? I shave my beard and moustache, even if it was Amitabh Bachchan style. I too scared to watch TV. Maybe I hear Muyazzumbhai is terrorist. Cannot trust anyone.

In school also, very quiet. People very scared… and ashamed. Muslim people very quiet. Betty teacher look sad, but she try to make us smile. But we too ashamed. I say sorry to her, on behalf of all Muslim people. She started to cry. Her friend also, killed in train. She say 'senseless massacre'. She say 'insane people'. She say 'threat to mankind'. I cannot understand big words but I know they are bad words. I feel terrible. I feel I am the terrorist who kill her friend. I will never go back to school again. But if I don't, they think I am terrorist and come to find me. What do I do? I am not free man anymore.

Am I threat to UK? I don't know. I have a wife who wore pink sari to airport and cried when I went. She is pregnant. So what? Bomber was assistant teacher in school and he had family. He was Muslim, like me. Am I a terrorist because I pray five times a day? I hide from the mirror. I learn a new word – *coward*. I have no job now. Royal B.C. is closed. It is now Polish supermarket called Ziomek. My classmate, Sylvester, working there now. He looked at me but not smile. Another coward. Do I want my son to be in this country? Maybe not. I don't know. In this country supermarket so big, is bigger than our railway station, I think. He will never be hungry. But he will never be proud man, always ashamed.

I know on those trains bombed, there were English, Polish, Italian, Welsh, Somali, Arabic, Indian, Pakistani, Bangladeshi ... and one terrorist with a bomb in his bag. Did he say 'good bye' to the passengers before he push the button? And in which language?

Good bye, my dear,

Hassan

Do widzenia. Ciao. Hywl. Nabadgelyo. Ma'a salama. Namaste. Khuda hafiz.

~

Susmita Bhattacharya was born in India. Her debut novel, The Normal State of Mind (Parthian) was published in March, 2015.

Letters Home was inspired by her experiences teaching English and Life Skills to immigrants, asylum seekers and refugees in Cardiff. She says, 'One day, I turned into a street that was covered in broken green glass. They twinkled like sequins into the distance. It was quite an astonishing view, almost like an art instalment. But I soon realised that this was the result of a night of revelry for the Welsh fans after winning a rugby match! They'd drunk all the beer and smashed the bottles to the ground. I knew this experience would find its way into a story, it just had to. Writing from an outsider's point of view at a new city came naturally, as I had experienced some of it myself, like the constant discussion about the weather and feeling tired just looking at the heaving shelves in the supermarket.'

A Ghost May Come
John Lavin

One eye. Just one. The pupil heavily dilated, the iris like a green beck collecting at the base of one of the mountains around here. Peering through a gap in the scarlet synthetic velvet curtains at the other side of the room.

I tell myself that it's just the candlelight disturbing the dark. The Burgundy with dinner and now the Muscatel with dessert playing tricks with the shadows. Playing tricks on my mind.

I've been here before. Once, five years ago. Once with you.

I wipe my mouth on the thick linen napkin and rise from my seat a little unsteadily. I walk over to the curtains. *Of course, there's no one there.* I draw them back with unintentional force, yanking one of the curtain hoops off the rail. The unnatural, vaguely metallic texture of the false velvet brushes against my skin like cobwebs, making me shiver. And then I'm opening the French windows and stumbling outside, cursing under my breath. Probably more loudly than I realise because when I turn to push the doors to, everybody in the restaurant is frowning at me from the other side of the glass.

My God. The sheer *sadness* of an autumn evening. The cold sky illuminated by a pale bright moon with the demeanour of some kind of ghost king in a big budget fantasy epic. A pale bright ghost king looking sadly over lands that had once fallen under his domain.

And the air is full of the fragrance of night frost and newly deceased leaves. It is a potion to open the past. Brimming my lungs with voices and faces from the past – all jostling for my attention – all of whom would beckon me back.

But there is only one voice that I can, in any case, ever *really hear*. Only one face that I can ever *really see*. Yours. My love. Yours, of course. Why else would I have come back to this place? To this hell on earth? Why else but to hear your voice ring out clearly? To have it cut through my despair and confusion like a bell pealing in the fog.

It was Halloween five years ago that I lost you.

Halloween. All Souls' Night. Samhain. A night with many names. Samhain simply meaning summer's end. *Summer's end*. Jesus Christ. It was that all right.

And now it is another Hallows' Eve and I have come back to find you. It is a ghost's night, after all. And did not Yeats say, in that poem of his that you loved – that incantatory poem, set on this very night – that 'a ghost may come'?

Yeats was your favourite. It was the Irish in you I suppose. Yeats, Kavanagh and Muldoon were always your favourites at university in any case. Where you studied literature with considerable success and I less so. Where we first met.

I set out on the path to the lake that we took five years ago. Retracing our steps. Going over and over again in my mind every detail of our last night together. Hoping to find what? Some clue? Some trace of your killers? Maybe partly.

But no. I am hoping to find a way to *invoke* you. To call you back from the dead.

Those two horse chestnut leaves. Red and gold. Almost radiant they seemed. You had sellotaped them into your diary after breakfast. Sitting outside with our coffees they had flown across and fallen straight into your lap.

Now it was evening and we were sitting inside by the fire, our coffees replaced with gin and tonics. I was staring, entranced, at the engagement ring on your finger. I had nervously treasured it for weeks. And you? You were writing around the leaves, recording our day. My heart was in the height of high summer seeing that glittering diamond on your finger. That glittering diamond which spoke to everyone of our allegiance. Of *your* unaccountable allegiance to *me*. I kept replaying it over and over again in my mind. The way that you had said 'well, *yes!*' and had then broken into a beatific smile.

To be able to make you smile like *that*. Maybe it was too much happiness. Maybe we had too much of our share too quickly. You looked up: your eyes beck-green, your hair bark-brown.

'Love *you*,' you said. Always so certain in your validations.

'Love *you*.'

You lit a cigarette and looked across to where the pine trees rose above the hotel drive. 'How about going for a walk after dinner? In the moonlight – *in the serious moonlight,'* you said breaking into a comic David Bowie baritone.

If only I'd said what I wanted to. *Why don't we just go to bed after dinner? Why don't we just make love?* But I was always shy. Always far too shy. And besides you were obviously suggesting the expedition for my benefit; suggesting it because we'd spent all day around shops and cafes when I had been hoping to do some hiking before we left west Wales for the north.

That sad-eyed Ghost King was up there already. Waiting for us in the rapidly emptying sky.

'Are you sure? It'll probably be freezing later, hun bun.'

Hun bun. Short for honey bunny. *Christ.* The pet names we used to come out with! It's too much to think of now. Too much to think in any great detail about how you then put your cigarette down, reached across and kissed me for just *the longest time.* So much so that I pulled away out of embarrassment in the end, knowing that we were not alone on the terrace of what was – and still is – a very expensive hotel.

'I can wrap up,' you grinned examining the long finger of ash that the expired cigarette had become; before causing it to fall felled-treelike into the ashtray with a single tap of your thumb on the filter. 'Come on let's *eat.*'

'I think there's a small lake nearby we could walk to,' I said, knowing very well that this was in fact the case. I had already examined an ordinance survey map of the area in some detail.

'Perfect, then!' you had smiled. 'We can ask the waiter.'

I had a dream about my grandmother the night she died. She came and stood over my bed, still wearing the floral nightdress from the hospital. Still wearing the horrible little plastic wristband they make you wear like you're going to a fucking festival or something. And she just laid her hand on my head and gave me a look that was... I don't know. I don't know if it was reassuring exactly because she looked tired and worried too. But I felt like she had come to tell me that she had died.'

You blew out a perfect smoke ring. 'In the morning Sal woke me up to tell me and before I knew what I was saying I said, 'I know.' And the thing is I *did*. I felt quite detached about it. And sort of lucid too. Almost as though Gran had given me an insight into the afterlife. I mean I just kept thinking – *how could she visit me in my sleep if she was just dead? If there was no afterlife?*'

You were throwing me a look of challenge then, your heart overflowing into your eyes, your lips tight in the smile-shape but not smiling. Expecting me to deny the possibility.

I gave you a reassuring look and moved my hand under the table to rest on your knee. You were wearing thick black tights I remember and a new dress that you had bought in Carmarthen earlier that day. Marks and Spencer it was from. Dark blue with red berries something like rose hips.

'It's funny though, isn't it?' you went on, still in something of a combative fashion. 'How you can think you're this amazingly rational person and then all it takes is one thing like that to shake your entire way of thinking? To make you believe in ghosts!'

'I know what you mean,' I replied. 'I try my best to think lucidly about God and existence and all of my thinking leads me to *not* believe in God or ghosts or... *whatever*. But even so I can't seem to help it!' I laughed. 'Peer under the surface and there it is. Mad superstition! Being brought up a Catholic doesn't help, of course.'

'Oh but for Christ's sake *I'm* not a Catholic, am I?' you had rejoined in exasperation. 'I mean *you've* met Roger and Sal haven't you?'

Your parents, Roger and Sal, still seemed a tiny bit

fantastical to me. Modern, liberal and resolutely atheist they were as far removed from the religious conservatism of my parents as I thought possible.

'The first time I met Roger and Sal they seemed like they'd accidentally stumbled out of the Bloomsbury group,' I smiled. "*What?* No one can have parents like this!' But no, I just mean that it's stupidly easy to be superstitious if you've been brought up a Catholic. I mean it's more like the other way round. It's more like it's fucking difficult not to be!'

Our voices had been raised for some time and the table to our side were now staring at me in open disapproval. You gave them your best, haughty private girls' school stare before turning back to me and affecting a particularly dirty smile. Then we were both suddenly giggling unstoppably. A feeling of reckless inebriation spreading between us.

And then I was wanting to tell you about something from years ago that had come into my mind from out of nowhere. I don't know why because I certainly hadn't consciously thought about that odd, sinister night for several years. But there it was unbidden and I drunkenly felt that I must tell you about it. I remember lighting a cigarette from the candle and you mock-tutting and reminding me that a sailor drowns every time that someone lights a cigarette that way. A Greek friend of ours that we lived in halls with at university had used to always chide us for doing that.

'There's this one thing,' I said. 'This one thing especially, that was weird and unaccountable.'

You moved your hand under the table and rested it on my thigh. Too much to think about that sensation now. Or to think in any detail about another evening earlier that week when you had sat beside me in the quiet backroom of an otherwise crowded pub and brought me to climax. A jacket over my lap and no time to take off the sharp-stoned ruby ring belonging to your grandmother that you always wore. The cold feeling of silver a little shocking after you had unbuttoned my fly. The faceted stone catching my foreskin from time to time, not that I cared.

'I must have been sixteen – fifteen even,' I said. 'It was the weekend and we'd all been getting pissed down the river as usual. 'You know the graveyard near my parents' house?'

You nodded. We didn't go to my parents' house all that often because we weren't allowed to sleep in the same room but you got on well with them all the same; even thinking of our separate rooms as being quite sweet and old fashioned. (I, on the other hand, was in the habit of flying into a rage with Mum and Dad about this.) I think you were the opposite of me in a funny sort of way; by which I mean that I think that you felt suffocated by liberalism and artistic freethinking in a peculiarly similar manner to the way in which I felt suffocated by my parents' religious conservatism. (Roger and Sal were extraordinary, of course, but as you would always say whenever I got too annoyed with my parents, 'At least they *care*. Roger and Sal just aren't really that interested.')

I continued: 'I was walking back home through the graveyard with a friend, when we saw two men drunkenly fighting and shouting by the side of the church. One man jabbed the other full in the eyes with his fingers. Really vicious. And this guy was just, you know, *clutching* his eyes, when the man smacked him full in the face and quickly again in the stomach. He tottered for a moment and fell backwards into what we suddenly realised was an open grave.'

'An *open grave?*' you queried.

'I *know.* Then the guy threw back his head and laughed in this really unpleasant, shrill way. Then he jumped after him into the grave!'

'Jumped *into the grave?*' you said, a look of disbelief crossing your face. 'Jesus, are you sure you're not making this up? I *do* know it's Halloween you know!'

'I knew you'd say that!' I laughed. 'But *no.* This really happened. We were both drunk ourselves it's true and, even, I will admit, a little stoned. But we *both* saw it. My friend insisted that we do something and so, even though – to put it *mildly* – self-defense was not a core strength for either of us, we both went over there, thinking that a murder might happen if we didn't do something.'

'Jesus, that was brave! What happened?'

'Well that's the strange thing. Nothing. When we got to what we were sure must have been the open grave, it was filled in. It was just an untouched old grave. And no sign of the men. And we *searched.*

'We couldn't understand it. I really can't understand it still. Where could they have *gone?*'

They remember me, of course, the ones who still work here. They do not acknowledge as much, nor are they pleased to see me, but how could they forget? The headwaiter, in particular, won't allow his eyes to meet mine. Doubtless he is afraid I will be full of questions and tears. That I will cause a scene.

It was he who told us the way to the lake. I can see him now, taking a liking to you. Gangling over our drunken heads, his icicle white moustache containing crumbs of food. His face helplessly taut, tied back by ill-health and worry-lines. He made it clear that he thought we were mad. The temperature had dropped and there was no outdoor lighting to speak of. But he fetched us a torch all the same. Beguiled, I felt, by the combination of your beauty and enthusiasm.

We walked up through the garden to the floodlit tennis courts. There we unlatched a tiny gate in a beech hedge and wandered out into the heavy country darkness. The torch revealed a narrow lane, an unkempt extension of the hotel drive. You slipped your arm through mine, saying:

'This is a proper adventure!'

For the first few minutes the moon was obscured by trees and we were quiet, reliant on the torch to be sure of our footing. Then we turned a corner and came to a small farmhouse. Somewhere within a dog began to bark and we both jumped. A light came on and, tittering like children, we went running hand-in-hand down the lane, into the valley. The Ghost King shining pale brightly over far-stretching fields. Disturbing their sleep. The dog ceased its barking and everything fell still. There were faint rustles in the undergrowth and the insistent whisper of the wind, moving across, animating the fields.

Our breathing amplified by the silence as we kissed.

'I can't wait to be Mrs *You*.'

'Mr *You*.'

Concentrating only on the movements of your tongue and the thoughts behind the movements of your tongue.

We were in a field then. Unconsciously unfastening. Unzipping.

A way to stop being separate. A way to lose all sense of what it means to be separate.

I ran across the field to piss. You sat up smoking,

pulling your tights up.

I ran a little too far, dazed by the wine and the intimacy and even enchanted a little by the moonlit, frost-glinting fields. I turned to wave but had come so far that I couldn't see you. I urinated noisily into a sheep dip, and suddenly all of the wine and rich food that we'd had at the hotel became too much for me and I felt an overwhelming need to be sick. I fell to my knees, trying to suppress the vomit with my hand.

I returned to you slowly, unsteadily.

But you weren't there. I thought that I must have gone the wrong way. A sliver of panic sloshed in my stomach. I retraced my steps and heaved a little when I reached the vomit-spattered sheep dip. No. I had taken the right way back. Now panic was coming in from all sides like water into a capsizing sailboat. But you had probably just gone off to find somewhere to go to the loo yourself.

There was no mobile reception out there. Not one bar.

I ran. It was no distance at all.

'Tash! Tash! Natasha!' I called.

Your name.

You weren't there. I stood over the indentation our bodies had made in the grass and scanned the shadow-shrouded wall that separated the field from the lane. I ran along it shouting your name. Then into the middle of the field. Shouting your name. *Screaming it.*

One eye, just one. Beck-green iris, the pupil heavily dilated. Calling me through the gate. The floodlit tennis courts disturbing the dark and playing tricks with the leaves.

Playing tricks on my mind.

They found you two days later. Twenty miles away. Washed up on a long stony beach outside Aberystwyth.

I went with Roger and Sal to identify your body. Your head sat rigidly on the slab. I wanted to say *forlornly* just then but that wouldn't be accurate because the body didn't really look animated in any way. It didn't, I mean, look *anything like you*. Rather, it looked more like someone had gone to the peculiar trouble of making a passable replica of you. You had been raped. Beaten about the face. Your right eye puffed out black-purple. Your cheek had been slit on the left side of your face with a knife. At the lip.

At the lip, so that it hung open a little. Like.... Like I don't know what. Like the most obscene thing that I have ever seen or will ever see again I suppose.

They never found your killers. Yes, the plural. It was two men the police thought. They couldn't be sure whether you were already dead before the men threw you into the water but probably not. Their investigations led nowhere. They found DNA traces on your body but they didn't match any records. The men seemed to have vanished into thin air, they said.

I walk along the lane in the thick, ungovernable darkness. Firmly, you take my hand. So certain, as ever, in your validations.

'Where have you been?' I ask. 'Tash?'

You will not say. And so we walk on in silence, down into the valley. The pale bright Ghost King looking down sadly over all these far-stretching, frost-luminous fields, that had once fallen under his domain.

~

John Lavin has a doctorate in Creative Writing from the University of Wales, Trinity Saint David. He is the editor of the short story anthology *A Fiction Map of Wales* (H'mm Foundation, 2014) and also the Fiction Editor of *Wales Arts Review* and former Editor of *The Lampeter Review*. His short stories have been published by *The Incubator*, *Spork Press* and *Dead Ink* amongst others. His latest venture, a magazine primarily devoted to the short story, entitled *The Lonely Crowd*, was launched this winter.

'**A Ghost May Come**,' he says, 'was the first piece that I wrote for the PhD in Creative Writing that I took at the University of Wales, Trinity Saint David. I was initially undertaking my work long distance; as a result I found myself living in Hove but very often thinking about Lampeter, the small University town in Ceredigion where I had also taken my BA. Writing the first piece for a PhD can be a little daunting and, my mind having gone quite blank, I decided to find a starting point by following the same principle that George Harrison borrowed from the I Ching for 'While My Guitar Gently Weeps'. In other words I opened a random book and used the first phrase that I came across. That book was *Horse Latitudes* by Paul Muldoon and the phrase the intriguing 'One eye. Just one.' In a sense, this phrase dictated the entire course of the story, as I immediately pictured someone peering through a gap in some curtains and began to wonder who the person was, why they were peering in etc. As I say, Lampeter was much on my mind, and so the grand hotel located there, The Falcondale, seemed a perfect location, partly for the simple reason of the long velvet curtains that I remembered having seen there but also because of its undeniably dramatic setting – situated as it is amongst woods and undulating hills at the end of a long drive.

Paul Muldoon also influenced the piece in another way, in that I had recently been reading his essay on Yeats' great Halloween poem 'All Souls' Night'. In that poem, of course, Yeats calls back the ghosts of dead friends, just as my narrator attempts to conjure his beloved Tash.'

Miasma
Karl Drinkwater

He kept his sarnies in his pocket, no appetite for food yet, stomach flip-flopping with excitement, dark hair pulled from his eyes, Dad's thick gardening gloves slipped on, sleeves tucked in, scratchproof. He checked to make sure no one else was in this thin bit of woods by the stream, especially adults, but it was just him and creaking branches overhead as vast green sails caught enough wind to bend stiff limbs; he hunched, careful in opening the box, dark crack inside, not big enough for escape – that had happened once before – then quick grab in, hold of fur, head, and now the cat squealed as he pulled it out; he licked sweat from his lips whilst getting a firm grip on the hissing, spitting creature, so much stronger than its size. He couldn't hold it up for long, so knelt by the water's edge and thrust it under, gripping with fingers pinched tight into muscle and folded skin while it struggled, bubbled, splashed ferociously with panic, he muttered "Just a test" but held it under, waiting for it to weaken before pulling it out; pushing it through terror to resignation, then offering the wet rag hope, heavier in his arms sympathetically tired, before he dropped it coughing and crawling in mud, maybe hoping it would live. It passed the test, and as he started to stab it with a pocket knife it bled into that mud, rich red, too tired to mewl loud, its voice not reaching the road beyond the wood, the road to the farm where the bull lay in bellows of pain, refusing to stand as it was kicked. "Its leg's broke," one man said, pointing. "Went through the grate, slipped." "We haven't got time for this," snapped the other, fetching the prod from the cabin. "Get up you lazy bastard!" It bellowed in ear-shattering vibration as he prodded it in the testicles again and again, cursing and kicking the useless animal. Further up, two miles away in the factory, blood and parts unsuitable for rendering were being sprayed down the gulley, high-pressure water merging with the dark-stained juices below chains as it blasted the floors from brown to red to pink to almost white before the next batch of lowing, panicked animals were dragged in. That blood and water filtered from the abattoir along artificial veins in the earth, dead, seeking rejuvenation in a heart that doesn't exist, filtering into mud stained brown, Earth's kidneys, washed out in streams and into the reservoir above, all town water filtered from there, micro-polluted with the essence of suffering, labelled "pure", into pipes, tanks, the tap he poured his glass of water from. He drank it then returned to the counter, woman with a boy, cute boy, dark hair in his eyes. "What you want?" the man asked, solid arms planted square. "Half a pound of ham for his sarnies." She rubbed the boy's scruffy hair. He flinched away uncomfortably, readjusting that dark fringe to hide his eyes and watching the cold precision of circular saw slicing thin cuts on to crisp paper, limp and dead and no longer struggling.

~

Karl Drinkwater has a switch in his head which toggles randomly between literary fiction, and dark fiction about chainsaws. Best not to startle him when he's working. He's currently finishing his latest novel,

2000 Tunes.

He says, "For many years I studied classics, particularly ancient Greek culture and language. **Miasma** was blood pollution, bad from bad, whether intention existed or not. It was a dangerous force, continually reworked by the tragedians, and tied to the nightmarish Erinyes; the rituals surrounding animal sacrifice showed the Greek uneasiness at any blood-spilling. Blood pollution worked in cycles. Once the bad things happened they kept happening in the same way – perverted killing, sacrificing and eating."

Disinhibited Limbic System
Justine Bold

Miranda stands alone, pale and pig-tailed in the playground on her first day back at school on a dry autumn day. It's break-time in a Monmouthshire primary. She's been away for ages. She doesn't know how long.

Her friends Medi, Lisa, Ben and Gwen won't talk to her. Neither will Sharon, Craig, Julie or Carol. Miranda tries to hold back the tears and doesn't understand. She sits on a step edging the pebble-grey playground where the white lines fade to dust. Dried leaves have collected at the step's edge. Around her children laugh, call and cry like gulls. A group of boys sing *'We're making plans for Nigel'*. A small boy, Nigel, with ruddy cheeks and stooped shoulders stands in the middle bemused and tearful. With his hands in his pockets he looks down and kicks at something on the floor.

Miranda watches Nigel and knows she is just like him. She tries to look occupied and grabs a handful of tiny stones to inspect. She drops the biggest onto the floor by her feet; one by one she lets go of the others. They chink on the faded tarmac, some thud as they hit the leather of her navy Clarks' shoes.

Julie walks towards her. Tall for her age with long mousey hair scraped into a thin ponytail. She doesn't yet know she will be plain when she grows up.

The other children are huddled together across the yard. They watch. When Julie is near enough to be heard she shouts to Miranda.

'You wet yourself.'

Miranda is silent.

Julie tries again.

'Your mum told Medi's mum, you wet yourself and passed out, that's why you had to go to hospital.'

'I didn't faint,' Miranda whispers 'I was sick.'

If Miranda tells Julie she had fits or it was her brain, she'll pay for it later.

Julie doesn't blink.

'But your mum told Medi's mum. You're a spaz...'

'It was a bug, a bad bug.' Miranda interrupts.

Miranda sits on the side of the avocado green bath at home and watches her mum and grandmother. Her mum is applying medicine to her grandma's toenails. The nails are discoloured and flaking: a fungal infection. Miranda thinks of rotting toadstools in the woods and screws up her face.

As she watches, her vision melts to tiny stars. Everything fades to black.

From inside the darkness where senses slip into nothingness, her mother cries out, 'Oh my god, she's having a fit.'

Miranda hears long after she can't see. Footsteps rush through the hall. Then the sounds fade, she loses consciousness and electrical energy pulses through her. She feels nothing as her body spasms.

She wakes with the family doctor at her side. He tells her she has to go to hospital soon and they don't know what's wrong. Miranda starts to cry.

She is in a white isolation unit. There are windows on two sides and a heavy door seals off the outside world. She's too tired to play and falls asleep with the other children visible through the door's round window.

Gwyn, her grandad visits the next day. He sits and holds her hand. Miranda is limp and tucked tight between white sheets. Her blonde hair is darkened and clings to her forehead. She's sleepy and drifts away. Each time she wakes, her grandad is still there. When he leaves, he kisses her goodnight with tears in his eyes.

Later Miranda feels sick and her mouth smarts. Fever is raging. The back of her head is wet and her hair is matted. Sore patches bigger than ulcers burn inside her cheeks. It's hard to eat. The doctor examines her, looks at her eyes, her mouth, ears, listens to her chest, asks her questions and studies the charts. Miranda listens as the doctor tells another doctor that they don't know what's wrong. Nurses take her temperature and bring foul-tasting pink medicine. She swallows and opens her mouth for the thermometer. The doctor says she's a good girl.

The next day, Miranda is still in the white room. The nurse gives her more medicine. Miranda swallows again. Minutes after the nurse exits, Miranda heaves and rushes to the sink where everything comes up. The thick yellow vomit stinks. The pink medicine is still visible. The smell stings her nostrils. Still nauseous, she cleans it away, poking the fibrous remnants down the plughole rinsing away all trace.

The nurse returns. Miranda's mum said she's from the Far East, perhaps the Philippines. Miranda tells the nurse she has been sick. The nurse is cross, Miranda washed the vomit away, she wants to see it. She scolds Miranda who's too weak to protest.

When her parents visit later that day they talk to the doctors. Miranda can't understand what they are talking about. A lumbar puncture. Her mum comes and hugs her. She explains; a needle might need to go into her back, between the bones, to get fluid. Miranda's mouth opens; she buries her face in her mum's skirt and sobs.

The next day, her mum and dad say no to the lumbar puncture. Miranda smiles for the first time since she moved into her white room.

The days slide by, long and empty; bound only by the edges of the ceiling and the round window. Brief moments break up the whiteness, visitors in pairs, mostly her mum and dad. They tell her Sally, her sister, is too young to visit so she stays with her grandmother. One day her grandmother and grandad visit again and they bring a new *Cindy doll*. Miranda's face lights up, she sits up straight, smiling. Over the next few days she plays with *Cindy* for hours.

A few days after she got her new doll, Miranda kneels on the hospital bed. *Cindy* is packed within a bag, her clothes are perfectly arranged. Excited, Miranda is dressed. The doctor says she can go home.

Her parents arrive with Sally. Through the round window Miranda sees them at the entrance to the ward. Her dad enters the room and hugs her. Together they gather her things. Then there are gappy smiles, hugs, a card and chocolates and for the nurses. She holds her sister's hand as she leaves the ward. Miranda checks to see if Sally is still smaller than she. Only fifteen months separate the sisters, after Miranda's illness and weight loss they are closer in size. Miranda is still taller, but the rest of her is about the same size. Miranda decides to eat more once home.

Outside in the car park, Miranda gulps down fresh air, holds it in, breathes out and expels the dry chemical smell of hospital. Her mouth tastes odd, but the air feels clean. It masks the staleness so she breathes deeply again. She's overwhelmed and laughs. Outside is busy; the colours bright and she can't focus. Noises and colours blur warming her cheeks. Miranda stands still for a moment, surveys the car park and skips towards a blue *Ford Cortina*.

Two days later in the early evening Miranda watches *Top of the Pops* in the living room, G plan is stacked against the walls. A lamp base made out of collected seashells sits upon the coffee table. Pebbles Miranda and Sally painted with varnish rest on the window ledge. Readers Digests sit in a row on the shelves.

In hospital, Miranda listened to the radio. Now she knows the words to her favourite songs. Tonight, *The Buggles* and *The Police* are on the TV. She sings, elated she can make a noise. Sally watches and joins in the chorus but she doesn't know all the words like Miranda. When the dancers appear, the sisters emulate the women on screen. Her dad looks in on them, tea towel in hand he smiles, happy to have Miranda home.

Her mum enters the living room and tells Miranda she has to go to have tests tomorrow. Brain tests. There might be brain damage from the fits. They need to know.

'I don't want to go. I don't. I'm better. They let me come home.

'Why Mum?

'But I don't need it, I'm fine.

'Can't you say I don't have to go?'

The next morning, they drive in her mum's silver car to the *special hospital*. Melville Hall. It's a long way from home.

Miranda fidgets and unwinds the window then closes it. She does this repeatedly. Her mum doesn't tell her off.

Miranda knows they are going to a bad place. Playground taunts have taught her so.

'I don't want to go, not there, please, please, please Mum.'

'We have to go love; I'll be with you when you have the test. It'll be OK.'

They arrive and Miranda sees a collection of budget bungalow prefabs. They park the car and find the entrance. Haphazard, dirty, corridors lead to nowhere. Miranda thinks the people look strange and sad. A woman screams in the distance.

The corridor smells. They see a man, his scalp flaky and bleeding. It's pitted with indentations the shape and size of fingernails. The man walks past them squeezed between two burly male staff. Miranda turns back to look and her mum pulls her forward. The man in uniform nearest to Miranda has dark hair on his forearms. The hair hides a large, indistinct blue-green tattoo. He doesn't look up. The other chaperone has a shaved head. The eyes of the man, pressed between are blank.

Miranda and her mum arrive at the room. Her mum knocks and they are called in. Miranda's heart thumps and she surveys the switches, knobs and a large screen. Behind this sits a thin man with hardly any hair wearing a white coat.

Miranda perches on a black chair in front of the man. He explains he's a doctor and she's having a test to see how her brain works.

She worries. What will happen if her brain doesn't work? Might she fail and get into trouble?

Miranda thinks of the wounds on the head of the

man in the corridor.

'Will I have a sore head?'

'No. It won't hurt.' The white coat replies.

Miranda watches the reflections in the glass screen before her. The man sticks red, black and white wires on her head with jelly. It is cold and itches as it dries. Miranda wants to pick her scalp. She fights herself not to and sits on her hands. Perhaps the man in the corridor picked his head.

It takes ages for the doctor to fix all the wires to her head. He works close to her and Miranda can smell his breath. It smells a bit like old sick.

The doctor steps away and Miranda is relieved as the smell fades. The man moves towards the bank of knobs and starts pressing some of them down. Lights flash, colours blink and sounds grind from machines. The test started.

It's nighttime after the test. Miranda's bedroom is decorated in pink wallpaper patterned with small flowers. The curtains and lampshade match. Her mum made them for her. In darkness, the inside of the room is black. Miranda awakes and sees a gleaming shape stands by her bed. Sleepy, she scratches her head and her fingernails find some of the dried jelly. She scrapes and flicks gummy remnants under the quilt as she hides from the shadowy figure. Sneaking one-eyed glimpses, she thinks her mum must have sent them to check if she's asleep. Pretending, she breathes deep and slow still peaking through the folds of the ironed cotton sheet. She can't tell if it's a man or a woman. It has blond curls, they are not long, but they are pretty. The air looks sparkly; the figure seems to glow. Surveying the rest of the room, it remains inky and dull. She's not seen anyone like this before. The muscles in her thighs stiffen slightly; her heart beats faster as she opens both eyes, tilts her head and stares directly at the figure. It stands close. She can see the folds of a gown glowing white, it's so near she could reach out and touch. She doesn't. Her hands remain under the sheet. The figure's hands held together, it seems it's praying. She swallows and looks again. She knows she should be afraid, yet she has no fear, none. She looks at the figure and then at its face. Seconds pass. Then she knows and feels sure. It's an angel. It's her angel come to see her. With her angel standing close, Miranda eventually falls asleep.

When she wakes again her angel is no longer there. Miranda gets up and walks to find her mum and dad. Their bedroom door is ajar so she pushes it open, 'Mummy, I've seen an angel.' Her mum stirs, sit up and she's out of bed quickly, walking towards Miranda as her dad still sleeps.

Her mum takes her back to her room.

'You've been really poorly. You must be seeing things. Maybe the temperature is back.' Her mum feels her forehead.

When Miranda is back in bed, her mum leaves the room. She returns moments later with a thermometer. She places this under Miranda's tongue and waits, then studies the reading. Her temperature is normal, 'It's O.K. You're fine. Night night. You must go back to sleep now. Sleep tight.' She kisses Miranda's forehead and tucks her in. Miranda looks into her mum's eyes; her Mum looks upset.

In the playground, Julie pokes a finger deep into Miranda's ribs. Miranda winces and wriggles away. Lisa and Medi snigger nearby, fascinated. Whispering

160

behind cupped hands as they stare, Craig, Ben and Gwen throw small stones towards her feet. Julie shouts, 'You peed your pants, peed your pants like a baby, urrgggghhh. You stink.'

Miranda shakes her head, 'No I didn't. I didn't. I didn't. I don't.' She takes a deep breath and leans away as she fights tears, 'I saw an angel.'

Craig and Ben look up and stop throwing the tiny pebbles, 'Don't be stupid. You're making it up.'

Lisa and Medi stand behind Julie. They gurgle like little witches, their mouths mean.

Miranda turns around. She walks away. She holds her head up and whispers, 'I saw an angel, my angel.'

~

Justine Bold's piece **Disinhibitied Limbic System** is a story that explores the gap between scientific explanation of psychic phenomenon and its lived experience. The story's title came from hearing a neuroscientist speak about brain activity. Justine has a broad interest in health and well-being is an academic lecturer in this field, but also has an interest in creative writing and is currently studying for the PhD at University of South Wales. Her work examines moments where science, medicine and life mingle.

Ingrid, Audrey and Jean
Diana Powell

When I was sixteen, I saw a man fall out of the sky. Then another. And another.

I was sitting on a beach in Devon at the time. Or Dorset. One of the clotted-cream, Enid-Blyton-for-grown-ups' counties. A 'nice' beach. 'Nice' featured a lot in our lives back then.

I wasn't supposed to be there. I should have been somewhere infested by bleached, feral sun-gods, or pot-smoking beach-bums, along with other teenage girls. Instead, there I was, reading 'War and Peace' – not Jackie Collins, nor even 'Lady Chatterley's Lover' – sitting beside my mother. Something else I shouldn't have been doing.

I don't know what made me look up. A shadow? A movement? A sound? A particularly tortuous paragraph in my book? There were plenty of those.

'Did you see that?' I asked.

'What?'

And what had I seen? It had happened so quickly. Perhaps I had been mistaken, and it was no more than the ramshackle tumbling of three crows across the cliff-face.

Or aliens. We had heard of such things, even in our safe little corner of England. Beings from other solar systems falling to Earth, intent on taking over our world, and our bodies.

Angels? But angels flew, didn't they? And were white. Or gold. Definitely not black... except, perhaps, for Satan.

And so I decided it must, indeed, be men. But how could it have happened? I had read, once, of a fridge falling from an aeroplane and landing on a solitary sheep in the middle of a field. The sheep died, of course. I think it was in America. Or Australia. Perhaps these men had fallen from a plane, too.

I got up. 'I'm going for a walk. To stretch my legs.'

Elsewhere on the planet, there was free-love and flower-power. People wore embroidered cheese-cloth smocks, ponchos, kaftans – if they wore anything at all. They decorated themselves with beads, bangles, petals, piercings.

My mother wore a twin set, even on the beach. She sat upright on a chair, brought to her by a 'man'. She was fond of getting a 'man' to do things for her, as if, somehow, added together, they would make up for the one that was her missing husband. Her shoes were her only concession to the sand – she wore sandals instead of her usual high-heels. But, still, walking was not part of her holiday agenda.

So I was surprised when she put down her magazine, and began to rise from her chair.

'There's no need...'

But she had started following me, sashaying wildly, as if the unfamiliarity of her footwear made walking far more precarious than five-inch stilettos.

And now, some distance in front of us, we saw dark shapes scattered at the base of the cliff, and knew, somehow, that they weren't rocks, or belongings abandoned by carefree swimmers. They, too, were something that wasn't supposed to be there.

Birds were beginning to gather around them. And then there were shouts and cries, and people running from the other side of the cliff. Sirens growing closer, louder.

'Come away,' said my mother. It was the same way she spoke to me when I was younger, when we were in the park, perhaps, and came across something 'not nice'. Couples kissing; rutting dogs; so many unpalatable tableaux of suburban life, all with the potential to contaminate. Once, worst of all, a flasher. 'Come away! Don't look!'

And I turned back with her, just as, back then, I hadn't looked. Because I knew, this time, at least, it really was something I didn't want to see.

I found out what had happened in the newspaper. There was no internet in those days. So no Facebook tributes, Twitter revelations, real-time photos taken by mobile phones. As it was, the information was scant. Enough, though, to tell me that it wasn't a man I had seen – none of them were. And they hadn't fallen from the sky. It was three girls, not much older than me. They had jumped together from the top of the cliff. I paused, then, in my reading. Why? It was the obvious question; the only question. Was it suicide? Or did they think they could fly, like Icarus and Daedalus... fly off the edge into the beckoning blue yonder, and on towards the sun? Or... what? They had been living with a 'family' in a big house a few miles away. The word 'commune' was mentioned. And the word 'cult.' But the people in the house said the girls had been quite happy there and were free to come and go as they pleased. There was no need for them to escape. There was no need for them to have done *this*. 'Escape' was the word that stood out for me from all the others. 'Escape' was the word I lingered on the most.

I dreamt about them that night. I dreamt about

them every night. Three bodies spiralling through space. Scarecrows cartwheeling downwards. Scraggy crows metamorphosing into androgynous humans.

They were not nightmares, as such. I never woke afraid, crying out, covered in perspiration.

After all, I had seen nothing horrible. True, I had watched three young girls dying, but I hadn't known it. And there was no blood, or gore, or grey brain matter spattered on the rocks below for me to witness. No. My mother's 'come away' had taken care of that.

In daytime, too, my thoughts would be full of them. I wanted to know more – so much more than the newspaper had told me.

Did they speak to each other as they stood there? Did any one of them have second thoughts? All? Did they hold hands? Yes – in my dreams, at least, they always clutched each other tightly, before some silent, unanimous signal sent them running towards the edge and their doom. And, at that final point of departure, suspended between solid ground and empty space, did they throw back their heads and laugh?

Round and round and round, variations of their final scene played through my head, like slides clicking from a film carousel. So many possibilities – a detail might change here, a whole passage of dialogue could be rewritten there. I swapped their faces around (for I had given them faces by then), interchanged with hairstyles and clothes, like a child's paper-doll dressing game. And then I gave them new names.

For I decided I didn't like the ones listed in the paper. They seemed too plain, too ordinary. So I rechristened them Ingrid, Audrey and Jean. Famous movie-stars, when film was the 'open sesame' to a world of magic – even my mother had fallen under its spell; it was her guilty pleasure. Hollywood was a fairy-tale realm, and its actresses the princesses who ruled there. They were not like us. And I didn't want the girls to be 'like us' either.

How long was it before I realised the stars were not of my own choosing at all? I had picked my mother's favourites. Actresses who also wore twin-sets, who had no scandal attached to them, who starred in tear-jerking dramas, or light romances. But, by then, I had grown used to calling the girls these names. It was too late to change.

In time, I left my dreams – and that day on the beach – behind. The girls hadn't died – I (and the newspaper) had been mistaken. After all, it didn't seem fair, they were so young, with so many years before them. I wanted them to have lives. So their faces became constant, and their personalities. And I made up stories about their pasts, their futures, and, most of all, their present. They were here, with me, now. It seemed the least I could do.

One day, my mother heard me talking to Audrey. She was my favourite – on that particular day, anyway. I was telling her she ought to change her hair – 'Get rid of the bun, Aude!' Or she was telling me. My mother stood in the doorway, and looked at us – me. She said nothing, and after a while, just walked away.

That afternoon, I found a newspaper spread out on the kitchen table. A big red asterisk was drawn by one of the headlines. It was an article covering the inquest and coroner's report of the girls' deaths. My mother had used her red pen to underline certain words, too. Drugs; hippies; sex.

My mother had decided that jumping off a cliff was something that happened to 'bad' girls. They were 'not nice'. And I shouldn't be mixing with them.

I didn't read the article. I didn't want to know more than I already did. Which was more than enough. Which was everything.

But, not long after that, I realised I was too old for imaginary friends. I knew that's what they were. I should have had them long ago, when I was younger. My mother might have welcomed them, then. So I said 'goodbye' to them – Ingrid, Audrey, and Jean – and wished them well. And decided that they were real, instead.

It was around this time that I went to work in a dress-shop in town. University was another 'somewhere' I was supposed to be (all that summer reading paying off, it seemed). But every time it was mentioned, my mother became unwell with some vague, unsubstantiated illness, and in the end, I just knew it wasn't going to happen.

The shop was the kind that sold clothes like my mother wore. It was a million miles away from Top Shop and Chelsea Girl; a whole galaxy away from Biba. But it could have been worse. The staff were kind to me. Every now and then, they would ask me if I would like to join them in a night out. I always said 'no', explaining I had plans of my own.

'It's the cinema with Audrey tonight,' I might say.

Or 'the four of us are going to Top Rank.' Back in work, they would ask me how my night out had been. 'Great!' I would say. 'We had fun!' And we had.

Once the four of us even had a week's holiday in Brighton, where the sun-gods and beach-bums lived. I spent the whole seven days shut in my bedroom and, the day before returning to work, applied fake tan.

'How was Brighton?' Marie asked.

'Fantastic! Fabulous! Everything I hoped it would be!'

Then I met Joe. He came into the shop one day, wanting a present for his sister. I wanted to tell him he was in the wrong shop. We got talking. I didn't mention Ingrid and Jean for the whole conversation. Not even Audrey. He asked me if I would like to go for a drink with him. And I said 'yes'.

I said 'yes', too, when he asked me to marry him. I knew I shouldn't have. I knew it was asking for trouble. I just couldn't quite see how.

For a while, everything went well. Even my mother seemed happy, and liked Joe. The girls disappeared. I told any of the shop-staff who asked that they had moved away. And, perhaps, if marriage could have happened without a wedding, it would have all stayed okay. But the day my mother and I went to choose my outfit, she said she was feeling unwell, and talked of her 'old troubles' returning. The night before, Joe had been talking of the possibility of a new job the other side of the country. And somehow, before I knew what had happened, I had chosen three dresses for my three bridesmaids. I had given their exact measurements, and chosen the right colour for their complexions. After all, I knew everything about them. And, later, when Joe called, my mother took him aside, and said something to him. And after that, he didn't call any more.

It's my mother's turn to go over the cliff, now. It's not the same beach – because, of course, I've never quite remembered where that was. And she won't somersault pell-mell over and over down to the bottom. She may never even reach there. The wind may catch her and send her up into the sky to be amongst the stars, or out over the sea, where she will float away. Or, if she should reach the beach, she will be lost amongst a million particles of welcoming sand. Dust to dust.

It doesn't matter what happens. I don't care. I won't be coming back; there will be no pilgrimages to pay my respects, visits to talk to her spirit. She's gone. At last. And that's it.

I'll walk back to the car, and drive away to a new life. Who knows – I'm not so very old. Anything could happen.

Besides, the girls are waiting for me there. Ingrid, Audrey and Jean. All of them, still. So I won't be alone. They'll always be there for me. *We'll* always be there. Together.

~

Diana lives with her husband in beautiful Pembrokeshire, where the siren-calls of the sea and her woodland garden conspire to lure her away from her desk. Fortunately, (or not!), the inclement weather of the far west helps her to resist temptation, and she has recently completed a novel, and is now working on a Young Adult book, plus a collection of short-stories about failed relationships. She has won several prizes for her stories, including the last PENfro for **Ingrid, Audrey and Jean**.

Of this, Diana says: 'Some years ago, I wrote a tale of three people jumping off a cliff. Almost immediately, I realised it didn't work, so relegated it to my bottom-drawer. But the opening image stayed somewhere deep inside me, to resurface – for some inexplicable reason – when I was reading an article about imaginary friends. The two ideas coalesced around the theme of escape, the word that haunts my narrator. I wrote the story far more quickly than usual, and I knew it was much better than my original effort, which proves, I like to think, that nothing we write is ever truly wasted.'

Fire
Luned DeSimon

The phone in her overstuffed bag was bleating every five minutes. Sarah looked around and under the raised table and seats, surveying the long stretch of perforated, dented grill running parallel to the train's stained carpet, but found no power sockets. Why run a commuter service from Holyhead to Manchester, with no power sockets? *It really is like a third world country*, she thought, hoisting her bag up onto the tabletop, and taking out the handset. There was no-one sitting opposite her to complain that she was taking up too much room.

The oblong phone display glowed cheerfully, despite the fact it was 8.32 pm. She was always so exhausted by this time of night; she never remembered to do the important things, like charging her mobile. She rubbed her smeary fingerprints off the face of the phone with the sleeve of her coat. She reasoned that it probably had enough power to last until she got home and she didn't like to switch it off in case the boys rang. In reality, she knew she would never get a call from one of them at this hour, unless it was a complete emergency. But because she had the thought at all, she decided to keep the phone directly in front of her; albeit behind the jacket of the book she was reading (*Ada* – her second and dogged attempt).

The train traced around the docks and the edges of the saltmarsh, blank-eyed with many windows, making a repetitive *clack-clack* sound. The light was pulling out now too, each day longer than the last, but there was still a cold in the wind that made no promises of spring. Even if the air was stale in the carriage, Sarah was glad of the seeping heat from the vent below and the tired, empty seats all around her. She had been more than happy to give up the family saloon, after they all moved out. It was only thirty minutes. The thought of breaking down anywhere alone at night kept her pleased to pay the rising railfares and put up with cheese and onion stink. And, the daily walks (which were admittedly, sometimes runs) for the buses to connect probably meant she was fitter than most of her office colleagues. She was usually home by now – no need for extra hours, slaving. No more dependents, although she still had the house to keep, for those much-anticipated occasions when they all piled back, smiling and hugging her to their broad shoulders. She stretched her legs to touch the battered seat opposite, and grinned at the thought of the three of them, each taller than the other with big men's hands and feet, clumsily smuggling Christmas presents into the house. It had been two years since the oldest boy and the twins had graduated, all in the same year, but she still struggled to cook for less than six people at any one sitting. It was a family joke, as well as instinct.

It was odd; she never felt strange about going back to the house, even after dark. She would get in, and turn on the heating, and the fume of the boiler sounded like breathing. Perhaps the residue of family memories meant she never felt alone. But she *was* alone. A long time and several scenarios ago, she had decided quietly that a non-existent husband was better than an ineffectual one. Strangers would wrongly assume her marital status from her age, or dress – she was fine with it. Her sporadic phone conversations with her sons bolstered her confidence that she had done "a good job" through all those years of blurry school runs, short-term charity positions, second-hand vehicles and overdrafts. The fact that the conversations happened just slightly less now, what with houses, girlfriends and careers, stood as proof that they really were equipped for life.

Still, Sarah sometimes felt creeping doubt, like a tell-tale patch of damp on a facing wall; usually when she was stood staring at the pile of ironing in one of the now spare rooms, or struggling with a minor repair. Had she been mistaken? Her girlfriends regularly told her not to be so stupid over the occasional drink or coffee, then, squinted to check their designer watches, got into cars they never needed to service, and drove perfunctorily back to what was usually a second or third marriage; wondering when she would grow up.

The train stopped somewhere in the sifting dusk. A sudden in-wash of streaming air and the pungent, familiar smell of bonfire drew her pleasantly from her thoughts. And then she saw them.

Two teens came into the carriage, with the subdued manner which often accompanies intelligent children who realise, on occasion, that all eyes are on them. They quickly scanned the seating arrangements. The tall lean boy swooped past Sarah, as a matter of fact, towards the back, while the smaller one sat only two rows ahead, on the same side of the train. They both wore dark-coloured tracksuits and sweatshirts, layered up against the wind. Sarah sensed their combined smell already permeating her hair; it was so strong, and sharp.

"Come sit here," called the boy from far behind,

after a moment.

"*You* can sit here, like," replied the other. As the child turned to drawl the phrase, Sarah quickly took in the forehead, the soft eyebrows and the small mouth, that hosted a chalky gleam of an overbite. There was also present, in that two-second reveal, the impossibly pure skin of a prepubescent girl. *A girl!* she thought. The petite head then turned nonchalantly back (ignoring him, Sarah noted) encased by a woolly hat, baseball cap, and soot-grimed hood over the top of it all.

The boy sauntered forward, and the girl made room for him without looking over. Fifteen, Sarah guessed. His hoodie was a bit grubby too, but pulled down around the nape of his neck. His translucent ears looked like someone had grabbed both of them and pulled, to see how far they would stretch from each side of his shaved head. The left one, much bigger, was punched through at the top with a silver ring. Both kids had similar plastic bags on double strings, the kind handed out after buying something in a sports shop, slung across their shoulders. The bags looked semi-full. He might have been a clear foot and a half taller than she was. They shifted slightly between them; then settled. Tearaways! It was darling, the way they were dressed similarly. *You and me against the world.* Oh yes, she remembered it well.

Sarah smiled, leaned back, half-closed her eyes, and settled in for a nice spell of people-watching, breathing in their cloying smoky smell deep to the back of her throat. They were obviously close, and he was in love with her. Yes. Protective, first love. Their amalgamated, radiating aroma made her think of long fields with overripe flowerheads, hiding in bushes, raiding sheds and yards for wood to burn, outdoor stories, and swigs of soon-to-be-missed-at-home alcohol. Wisps and hints of her very favourite things she first discovered in youth (before she fell pregnant, barely out of it herself). It was no matter – these she had been able to re-assemble lovingly, in safer format, for her boys coming into their own as teenagers, and their friends (usually ignored by their parents) on rugby tours and camping trips. Without the drink, of course; she left them to get on with discovering that themselves. The unruly years! There were some places she just couldn't go, as their mother.

There was something gratifying about the way the tall boy dipped his head towards the girl every few moments, smiling at something she commented on. The train was too loud to catch their conversation, but the body language was one of quiet and adoring supervision. That's nice, Sarah thought to herself, happy to find a pair of teenagers that met with her approval, by chance, in a *let's face it*, rough section of the North Wales coast. She turned her head back to her book, smiling. After just a few pages, the train was wheezily pulling into the station where she could catch her bus home.

The youngsters got off too, just ahead of her, and Sarah slowed her progress from the platform to allow a respectful distance. The height difference was so marked now that they were walking in front! The girl really did look like a boy, stepping with her Converse-shod, slightly in-turned feet; him walking nearly two paces apart, and just forward. The intimate looks were nowhere now, being out in public; and Sarah couldn't help wondering about where they were going, and what their future held. She was already on the far side of the railway bridge, and they had turned away from her to walk to an adjoining platform, when she thought: *they probably didn't want to attract any attention*. She smiled to herself. Then, the repetition, in her brain, of this concrete fact raised the hairs on both her forearms, and stopped her where she stood. *Holyhead*.

Suddenly, a ticking memory of a port-side news feature floated up in her consciousness, like a name she had been struggling with all day. It was late, and she was tired. What was it? – a sense of movement, of border – an absence. Like the curt term her sons batted at her when she struggled with trivia games during the holidays. *The weakest link.*

Children. Holyhead.

Gone.

She immediately felt like she had swallowed lead. Her bus was waiting across the road while she swayed, gaping and watery-eyed, in the doorway of the station. She turned, and ran back.

There were never guards on anymore at this time of night. Cutting overheads saw to that. There was no one to call out to; no one to help. Her heels scraped each granite step as she pushed her middle-aged, out-of-shape body up and across the bridge, her bag banging against her legs, her heart flashing up the only phrase she could sensibly articulate if anyone had stopped her: *She's too young! She's too young!* She might catch them. Her phone was still in her coat pocket.

She was coming to the bottom of the bridge, and stopped dead to scan the empty platforms in both directions. Her vision strained and flared against the lucent train windows; it was the last few minutes before nightfall. There was not a soul looking back at her, there was only the sound of her heavy, futile breathing. Nothing. Then came the fizzy definitive pop of her mobile giving up the ghost; reminding her that her natural state was to be never, ever, responsible enough.

~

Luned DeSimon writes fiction and scripts and lives and works in Flintshire, North Wales. Her stories have appeared in several literary magazines in the UK and North America and she is working towards her first collection with support from Literature Wales.

She says: 'The idea for **Fire** came from a report about Welsh ports being used as "soft targets" for human trafficking that I absorbed in 2012/13 when I was writing a story about motherhood, and childhood. Actually, the story started as a response to a call for an anthology of ghost stories, which I think is poignant to note. The mechanics of my creative process is also central to the story. As a writer, I don't say much, I watch out. And when you really do watch, the mundane becomes indelible; it's a very natural part of being human.'

Theft
Bethany W Pope

Time is a slow but steady thief who slips in through the window or under the door and leaves, every night, with a brown bag clutched under his arm, bulging with another slice of your life. Dylan kept catching glimpses of him in the insomniac shadows he became so familiar with; the aching quiet of four AM.

First, Time took the apple trees Gwen planted in the first year of their marriage. The leaves went yellow, one by one, and the fruit bulged with wasps instead of seeds. Then, Time took the English Vicar who learned Welsh to wed them, at their request, and stumbled (sweetly) over the simplest phrases. Time took the children, of course; off to school, then out to Swansea (which might as well be London for how rarely they come home to visit their old Dad).

These trespasses were expected, and forgivable. Dylan winked at Gwen as she poured out his coffee, glad to finally be alone together after many years of diapers, screaming, and nights of interrupted lovemaking as three small bodies wriggled between the two of them, crashing into a bed made crowded by sticky stuffed animals, sweet breath, and the residue of simple, childish nightmares.

But then time took Gwen.

That theft was less funny.

Dylan started paying attention. He stopped sleeping much. All food tasted poorly, so he cut back on his eating. He noticed soft-soled Time sneaking round more and more often. Time visited as often as a friend. He stole inches from Dylan's stomach and curls from his head. Time's black, shiny eyes gleamed from the shadows above the refrigerator the night before the dog went missing (leaving behind a collar, an empty bed, and a few lone strands of long, wiry fur) and Dylan knew for sure that it was not the new moon, but Time's white teeth that shone (sharp and white as a cat's) through the window the night Time drained the strength from Dylan's arms. Dylan caught Time toting the last of his old man's might, bottled away in a jar made for cider.

Dylan watched the small man running up the road, his jar gently sloshing, and wondered what it tasted like, this draught of his youth. He imagined it was sweet, with a little intoxicating bite; a potion powerful and good, like pulped, fermented apples.

Dylan couldn't stand to watch his own slow reduction, the slow divestment of his self. He sat at the warped pine table he'd carved and hammered long ago and thought as hard as he could, staring at his brown-speckled paper-skinned hands, striving hard to find a new and better vision. His long, thin fingers looked like winter branches, crooked, bloodless, and cold.

One night passed, one day, and then another. Dylan drank cup after cup of air-cool coffee. He couldn't recall ever refilling the pot. Time looked out from under the table, laughing through his needle-like nose.

'Son of Man,' Dylan asked himself, 'can these bones live?'

Dylan was not one to think, much or often, about God. He did not presume to know if there was a place called heaven, but he thought there was, and that he'd touched it, once or twice, when he wasn't paying attention. Now, in a room so silent that the dying flies the spiders caught screamed almost loud enough for Dylan to hear them, the old man fought the retreating tide of his pulse to haul those moments back again. He thought about green buds forming on old, tired branches. He pictured a soft, wrinkled cheek plumping and smoothing, ripening in reverse, gaining colour and the sweet, powdery fragrance of female youth. He closed his eyes and buried his nose into the soft, yeast-scented pads of a puppy's untried paw, and cupped his hand about the tender, easily bruised skull of an infant that he was, at one point, too terrified to hold. And all the while, Time was laughing, joyfully laughing, as he gathered up the image of a lonely old man, asleep at a table in a puddle of sun.

~

Bethany W Pope is an award winning writer. She is the author of several collections of poetry: *A Radiance* (Cultured Llama, 2012) *Crown of Thorns,* (Oneiros Books, 2013), *The Gospel of Flies* (Writing Knights Press 2014), and *Undisturbed Circles* (Lapwing, 2014). Her first novel, *Masque,* shall be published by Seren in 2016.

She says, 'I wrote **Theft** at three in the morning in my grandmother's kitchen while exercising on my portable stepper and longing for sleep to come and collect me. It never did. The story caught me instead (with the image of an empty dog-bed) and the next thing I knew, the sun was rising and the night had fled. The fact that I had been spending a lot of time with people who were actively preparing for death forced me to consider what it is like to know the thing

that's coming for all of us, and to lose, slowly, all of
the beauty that we thought we had. I set it in a
location based on the home of a friend who lives in a
small town near Aberystwyth. Her home is one of the
loveliest places that I have ever seen, and therefore it
is sweetest and also the bitterest place to visit. Beauty
always comes with a date of expiration.

Maria's Silence
Carly Holmes

Maria was perched on the back of the stone horse. Cross-legged, chin in palm, scowling into the distance. The early risers, humming their way wearily work-wards, saw her first. They jumped and blinked and let out yelps of wonder. They turned and ran, or approached on tiptoe and reached out a trembling hand to touch her foot. Stroked fingertips through nothing.

She sat and scowled and ignored them all.

Somebody thought to fetch her parents and somebody else thought to boil up a kettle and sell hot tea. Before the morning sun had even started to warm the chill stone flank of the horse, the town square was thick and writhing with bodies. The church bells grumbled above their deserted shell.

Her mother, when she arrived, broke apart and poured grief in salty shrieks onto the horse's hooves. Her father stood rooted to the flagstones and had to be carried home in the arms of four men: a cardboard cut out.

Her best friend ran to join the throng, shiny with hope and love, panting with exertion.

"Maria?" she called. "Is it really you? Have you come home?"

Maria turned her head a little, and sighed, and continued to scowl.

"Maria, please! It's me, Anna. Come down and talk to me, tell me what happened. We thought you were dead!"

Anna began to weep. People looked suspiciously around, anticipating a cruel and tasteless prank. The grocer and the butcher began to argue with each other and the postman's dog started to whine. The sun groaned and heaved its swollenness higher into the sky.

Anna scrambled up onto the horse's plinth, clambered over its timeless trot, and swung herself with a cry of triumph into its saddle. She flung her arms out to embrace her friend.

"Don't ignore me, Maria!"

Her hug collapsed through the air as if through honey and she lost her balance. Men leapt forward to catch her as she tumbled from the horse and jostled with each other to clutch her famous curves. Maria narrowed her eyes and blew a wisp of hair from the corner of her mouth. She uncurled her long legs, stretched, and resettled herself.

Anna jerked her flesh away from the men's clammy pinches and straightened her dishevelment. She shivered and pointed.

"It can't be!" She turned to the people standing, staring. "Did you see? I couldn't touch her. There was nothing to hold onto!"

And she knelt and covered her face.

Maria shrugged and gazed moodily over the terrified screams. She began to bite at her fingernail.

By lunchtime Maria's mother had returned, though her father remained in their kitchen, where he'd been carefully set down. Strings of onions now dangled from his frozen wrists and several sun hats crowned his bushy head. An energetic card game was taking place around him.

"Speak to her, Isabella. Ask her what she wants!"

Maria's mother was nudged through the crowd. When grief burned the words from her lips, elbows jabbed impatiently at her ribs.

"Maria? Are you a ghost? Have you come home? Do you want me to make you some coffee? The stove is lit, Maria, and your bed is made up, ready…"

Her words fluttered around like torn paper, swirled on the breeze across the crowds, and floated past her daughter's face. Maria pouted out her lips and blew the words away. She turned her head slightly and her mother's trembles were no longer in her sight line.

Elbows crooked and created hard angles, swung into readiness, and Isabella wrapped her arms around her tender spots and hastened on.

"I want you to come back with me, Maria, and tell me what happened. Shall I bake you some gingerbread? Would you like that?"

Everybody shuffled and whispered. Somebody giggled.

The cobbler's wife, a woman more ancient than the tooth fairy, shuffled forwards and glared upwards.

"Do as your mother tells you! And don't forget that I've still got your last pair of dancing shoes in my shop, re-heeled and waiting to be paid for."

She brought her cane down, hard, on the flagstones, and the people nearest to her jumped and gasped. Maria flinched but kept her scowl in place. The cobbler tutted.

His wife shook her head and held up a twisted hand.

"Right! If you don't come in and collect them by next Wednesday then I'll have them myself, or put them in the window. There're plenty of others who'd like the chance to own such a well-made pair of shoes."

She began to move away.

"Come on! All of you. Leave her to think about *that*. Red leather they are. Lovely. She'll soon come round."

The townspeople trailed reluctantly in the choppy wake of her limp. Maria's mother waited until they had all left and the square was empty of everything but the high-pitched backwash of chatter. She stood beside her daughter and cupped her hand around the emptiness of Maria's ankle, memory finding the delicate bone there and stroking it.

"I'm just glad you're back, my love. We'll be at home, waiting, whenever you're ready. I'll make a start on the gingerbread right now."

She sniffed and squeezed the air before releasing it. There was a second's silence, and then she started to wail.

Maria swallowed. She stared over her mother's head and readjusted her scowl.

Day after day, Maria stayed on her stone perch, gazing at the muddle of cottages surrounding her, or at the distant sea, draped like a spangled shawl across the horizon. People started to lay gifts around the horse, approaching sheepishly and departing quickly, or lingering to take a look at the offers on display. Flowers, bowls of milk, and dried sausages appeared and disappeared. The florist's cheeks grew fat and the butcher always had a pink rose in his buttonhole. When the dairymaid appeared every afternoon with her two pails, she was greeted with impatient muttering and the tap of spoon on tin mug.

When squabbles broke out over the last fresh roll, Maria ignored all requests to mediate. The tooth fairy's grandmother returned on one occasion, swollen feet howling inside scarlet leather, and had to use her cane to prod apart two elderly men who had both dived on a plate of scones, each refusing to surrender their claim. She delivered energetic stripes to their backsides as they squealed on the ground and crammed their pockets full of cake.

After that incident, a ban was placed on all offerings and instruction given that no more than five people would be permitted to congregate at the town square at any given time. After some confusion and disagreement it was decided that this rule be amended to specify only living people, at least until the questions surrounding Maria's mortality had been satisfactorily answered.

Isabella ensured that she was always one of the no more than five. Each morning, after she had prepared the breakfast and sent Katya off to school, she took her clothes off and tried for an hour or so to overcome her husband's catatonia, swirling and shimmying before his fixed stare, and then she packed a basket with warm bread and hot chocolate and set off to spend some time with her eldest daughter.

"Today will be a good day," she would mutter to herself, as she walked. "Today she will talk to me." And her smile would firm and brighten, her back straighten with a mother's pride, as she turned into the main street and spied Maria's shadow-less silhouette.

Anna was often there and when the two women met they would embrace and raise eyebrows, shake heads and sigh. They shared the contents of their lunch baskets, carefully divided between three plates, and they sung songs, exchanged scurrilous gossip, or filled Maria in on what had changed in the town over the last year, since she had 'been away'.

Maria never turned her head to acknowledge even the juiciest piece of news, though her scowl deepened and lightened in rhythm to the chatter, sometimes almost lifting clear into the sky and darting up to the clouds before swooping back down to her face.

One afternoon Anna brought along Maria's death certificate and held it up in front of her friend.

"Look. Just take a look at it. It says here that you died on May eighteenth, two days before your nineteenth birthday. Do you remember? Please tell me, Maria. Why are you here?"

She drew breath and continued on with raised voice.

"Did you know that I found you? Did you know that? You were just lying there on the beach, no mark on you, and I thought you were asleep. But you wouldn't wake up. And then the doctor said that you'd taken tablets. Have you come back to tell us why? Are you angry with me? You are, aren't you? Please talk to me, Maria."

Maria rubbed the side of her nose and began to pick at a loose thread in her dress.

"Maria, please! Think of your mother and what she must be going through. She's used up all the sugar in the village with her baking and the hens are exhausted from laying so many eggs. If you won't talk to me then I'll bring paper, and a pencil, and you can write it down. Will you do that?"

Two young boys wandered past and paused in their whistling to stare at the famous ghost. One nudged the other and hefted his half eaten apple to shoulder height. Drew back his arm and sniggered.

Maria twisted on the horse and bared her teeth.

The boy's screams blew them right out of their

school trousers and raced neck and neck with them all the way home.

"That has to be a good sign. Don't you think that's a good sign?"

Isabella stopped slapping her husband's face. She began to twist his nose.

"She reacted to the boys. She scared them off. Maybe she's ready to talk... Oh come on, Gabriel, at least make an effort to snap out of it! My hands are sore from massaging you and I'm starting to suspect that you're enjoying being spoon fed more than you're letting on. I've got a good mind to leave you in the cellar and see how that suits you..."

She gave his ears a quick, sharp tug and then released him and turned away.

"I'm going to fetch my knitting now and go back to the square. Don't expect any dinner and don't wait up for me. Katya's with the neighbours. Oh, and there's plenty of cake if you get peckish."

She bustled from sewing box to kitchen cupboard and then jerked open the front door and hurried out, slamming it behind her. Rays of early evening sunshine which had been pressed up against the door, jostling for a turn at the keyhole, lost balance and spilled across the kitchen floor, before picking themselves up and darting into the gloom under the table.

Maria refused to grip the pencil she was offered and she refused to whisper in her mother's ear. She plaited and re-plaited her hair, counted the freckles on her arm, and began to wipe clean with the sleeve of her blouse an area on the horse's neck.

Isabella lost patience.

"I've had enough of this! I know you can hear me

and I'll bet you can talk to me, so why won't you make the effort? How can I help you if you won't even tell me what the problem is?"

She waited.

"Would you like the last piece of date loaf?"

Maria continued to rub.

"Fine. If that's the way you want it... But I'm not going anywhere. I've got my knitting and a flask of tea, and I'll stay here day and night if need be, until you decide to speak."

Isabella wrapped herself up against the chill and sat on the ground, huffing and muttering. Her hip quickly started to ache and she began to moan bad temperedly. Her knitting needles clattered as she worked out her frustrations on a jumper for Katya. Above her, Maria shifted in her saddle.

The evening shrunk and leapt into the arms of the night, which cradled it and then set it aside. The moon shivered and drifted across the sky. The tooth fairy's grandmother clattered from shop to home in her new red shoes. The butcher, the grocer and the blacksmith drifted into the lamplight around the square, to laugh and banter and snatch peaks at the girls walking by.

Doors slammed and windows trembled in their frames. The men finished their drinks and shouted their goodbyes. The girls pouted and stopped tossing their hair. Flowers folded in on themselves like fallen ballerinas. Cats shed their daytime personas and danced with the shadows, practised their spells. Isabella dozed for a while.

When she awoke, she was cupped in the palm of deepest night. For a moment she felt the panic of childhood but then she raised herself and looked around her, probing the thick layers of jet until she could see the stars. She glanced up at Maria but couldn't make out her features. The world was asleep. The silence was complete. Joy settled on her.

And then she heard it. The absence of noise, and beneath that, her daughter's voice.

"Mama, can you hear me now?"

Isabella threw herself against the stone flank of the horse and began to sob.

"Maria! I can't believe you're finally speaking! Talk to me! Tell me how you are! Tell me everything!"

Maria covered her mouth. She closed her eyes.

"Maria! Speak to me!"

Isabella fed her grief with howls until it peaked and burst. She collapsed onto her knees and nodded her head. Gave her daughter silence. Maria opened her eyes and rested her hands back in her lap.

"Thank you, Mama. I came back to tell you that I'm sorry for what I did, for hurting you all. And I came back to tell you that you must give Katya silence once in a while. Let her be quiet when she needs to be, and listen to her pauses as well as her words. Please do that for her, so that she doesn't become me.

"I must go now, I've stayed longer than I should, and it's tiring me as much as it ever did to have to compete with the noise of this world. I've been speaking to you the whole time I've been here and I've been waiting for you to be silent so that you could hear me. I love you, Mama."

She reached out and traced a finger across her mother's cheekbone, though neither of them felt it.

She smiled.

~

Carly Holmes is a novelist and short story writer who

lives on the west coast of Wales. She manages and hosts The Cellar Bards in Cardigan, and is a strong supporter of Welsh and Wales based writers. www.carlyholmes.co.uk

She says, 'The genesis of *Maria's Silence* came, as a lot of my fiction does, from a sudden image that flashed before my mind's eye. I was driving through Aberaeron, past the horse statue by the playing fields, and imagined a young ghost girl sitting on it, ignoring the passers-by in a singularly unconventional haunting. I pondered on this for a while – Why was she silent? How had she died? I've always loved magic realism and writing which, while having a fantastical edge, also has a serious point to make, and so I took the ghost girl and relocated her to an unnamed village with a cast of almost fairytale characters, all of them noisy. Even the landscape won't be quiet. As the story unfolds the reasons for Maria's silence are revealed as a need for silence in a world which doesn't allow for quiet.'

Boy 8 ¾ Squares Away Robbers
Nic Herriot

'**H**is mummy's going to die.'

'What did he say?'

'Nothing, he said nothing he is just a little boy.'

'No mum, look, it's bad luck, look at where he is standing.'

'What? What about where I'm standing?'

Jamie aged 8 and ¾'s stood up and approached him with a worried look on his face. His Mum looked scared and made to grab and stop him. Jamie stood opposite the man. The man, Danny, looked nervous, this wasn't in the plan. He didn't need to look nervous, after all he was the one wearing the balaclava and carrying a sawn off shot-gun.

'You're stood on two squares; you should be in just one,' Jamie moved Danny's legs by gripping his jeans, 'and your arms, they overhang, bring them in a bit.' Dan's shotgun stance so tough, so practised before, was now neat and tidy with his gun pointing downwards. The other balaclava clad bank robber, for that's what they were, bank robbers, looked worried and shuffled his feet so he too, took up only the one square on the grey tiled floor.

The other customers were scared and not able to comprehend what was happening. They had been shocked into obedience when the three men had burst into the bank yelling 'SIT DOWN. SIT DOWN ON THE FLOOR. NOW.' Some of them dared to look up and see the small boy with the dark curly hair talk to one of the men. Jamie's mum shuffled forwards as if to bring Jamie back to safety always making sure she was contained within one square, but stopped when the second bank robber, Jack, moved closer to Danny.

'What does he know about our Gran, what's he saying?'

With the stress of what they were doing Jack had misheard, because they were doing this for their Gran she was uppermost in his mind... that and the fact that if she found out what they were doing she would skin them alive, sew them back up... only to skin them alive again.

They needed money to move their Gran into a care home that was better than the one she was now in. Their eldest brother, Mickey said they weren't looking after her like he would've and suggested they rob the bank to pay for a new home for her. What the two younger brothers didn't know was that Gran had no intentions of moving anywhere else and Mickey planned to keep the money for himself. Even under the illusion the money was to help their Gran they still weren't keen, but Mickey was insistent. He had made them watch *Lock Stock and Two Smoking Barrels* as part of their training. He wanted them to be tough, have attitude. Danny and Jack just saw lots of people getting killed, something they wanted nothing to do with. They had to have 'gang names' so that no-one would know their real ones to tell the police afterwards. The trouble was that both Danny and Jack, or Dagger and Scarface, couldn't remember their new names and their conversations were peppered with 'Dan-dagger' and Jac-scar.

Their weapons weren't even real. They had gone down to Camden Market to buy replicas and they had taken a fancy to the 1800's pistol they had found, as they both wanted to be Capt'n Jack Sparrow. A scuffle had broken out until the stall holder had pulled them apart. Mickey didn't know about the incident and thought the black eyes were because they were finally taking him seriously. He thought they had watched *Fight Club* or had gone to the local boxing club without his prompting. In the end the brothers had chosen modern styled weapons, plastic to look like metal and had cut off the red ends to make them look realistic. They even fired red plastic bullets... that's if they had been loaded. Danny and Jack didn't even want to go that far.

Jamie looked at them, his smile broad now he saw that the men were being safe again.

'You have to be careful, don't go over the lines, and you have to keep one square from each other, that's how it works.' Jamie took his time to organise the other customers so they were the correct distance apart, telling them that to do it properly you had to move up and down and not cross at the corners.

That was when the police arrived.

Danny and Jack's sister had refused to take part in this crazy scheme so with no getaway driver, the car was parked outside on double yellow lines, but Danny had left the hazard lights on, to be safe. The traffic warden had given it a ticket but now it was causing havoc as a lorry couldn't get past and the traffic had backed up throughout the one-way system, the town was on the verge of a gridlock. The police had been called to help find the owner and manage the irate drivers and as it was outside the bank it was their first port of call.

The two uniformed officers had wandered in expecting to find the driver in a long queue. As they opened the door they knew this wasn't the case. They saw the men with guns and instinctively reacted to the scenario and entered cautiously but became confused as everyone started shouting at them not to step in certain areas. A bank assistant approached them and told them how and where they could move pointing to a small child who seemed to be with the gunmen. Every time the officers moved people were yelling at them, including the robbers who seemed to be giving themselves up as their weapons were now on the floor. Several of the customers were giggling in near hysterics as the senior of the two officers strode over and took command of the situation.

The Officer pulled out his handcuffs to apprehend the two tearful young men, but neither Danny nor Jack would put their arms out, mumbling something about their Gran would die if they went over the lines. They would put an arm out but only a short way and then would panic and pull it back. The other police officer was trying to whip one cuff onto a wrist as it came close to him. He was negotiating with Jack as to whether he could give the handcuffs to him to cuff himself, whilst also keeping one square away as every time he moved closer the entire bank erupted into screams of panic. Jamie was stood near Danny trying to help, in the way only an 8 and ¾ year old boy can.

At that moment two things happened. From the front entrance came the sergeant, fed up with waiting outside for his two men to reappear, after all how long does it take to find one driver? And from the staff door came the manager and the third robber.

The manager was pushed to one side as Mickey, rucksack over his shoulder stepped forward trying to understand what was actually happening.

'Mickey – don't move, it's bad luck,' shouted both his brothers, forgetting they should use their gang names. He cursed loudly as he realised his stupid brothers had let him down again. Sgt Taylor immediately recognised Danny and Jack as they had long ago taken their balaclavas off so he knew who the hooded man would be without their shouting his name.

'Give it up now,' he commanded as Mickey lifted his shotgun up. Everyone else went silent. Jamie went to move towards Mickey to make him safe but Danny grabbed him up into his arms and held him tight to his side, hiding him from Mickey, both tight within the one square putting a finger to his lips telling him to be quiet as well.

Mickey stepped forward his gun aimed at Sgt Taylor.

'Don't make it worse for yourself Mickey, give it to me now.'

Both brothers were also yelling for him to put his gun down as they had had enough excitement for the day and just wanted to go home. Although Mickey had the only genuine weapon Jack had managed to remove the ammunition that morning when it was left on the kitchen table but with everything going on he was worried things could get worse and Mickey would be shot by the police.

It did get worse.

From behind Sergeant Taylor came a small old lady on the arm of her granddaughter.

'Granny!' the happiness that Danny and Jack felt at seeing their Gran unharmed and here was unbounded. Gran, or 'Mrs Holloway to you' as she often scolded the staff in her care home, took a sweeping look around and saw Jamie's mum who gave her a weak smile in return. Mrs Holloway recognised her as Harry Sullivan's granddaughter. She then moved neatly into one square as she knew Jamie must also be around here somewhere. She and Harry met every month in their local cafe remembering old times and chatting about their families. She knew all about Jamie's problems, and whilst she held no truck with this modern malarkey she knew all about difficult children and she knew how fond Harry was of his granddaughter and great-grandchild.

'Mickey!' commanded Mrs Holloway as she kept walking forward. 'Put that bloody gun down you idiot! Hello Sgt Taylor, how are you? How's Mrs Taylor?' She nodded to the sergeant who, whilst returning the greeting with a salute was relieved that she had arrived as she was the only one who ever could handle Mickey without a fight and handcuffs. He was also working out his statement so the others at the police station wouldn't think he had been rescued by a pensioner. By now Mrs Holloway stood in front of Mickey and took a swiping blow at his knees with her walking stick. That was the final straw for him and he meekly laid his gun down.

Both the other brothers held up the hands to be cuffed, after all, it didn't matter now, their Gran was safe, and were led out by their corresponding police officers. Mickey was cuffed and held firmly by the sergeant and taken away with Mrs Holloway, berating him with her stick.

Jamie ran to his mum who hugged him tight, relief making her crush him. 'Mum, lines,' he squeaked. She released him to the applause of the others who moved around trying to congratulate him on stopping a dangerous situation from getting worse.

The next week after making the local news

headlines the national media tried to cover the story but Jamie and his mum were not interested and refused all interviews. He was happy being with his Great-Granddad visiting that fierce lady at her care home, after all he had been promised a Knickerbocker Glory afterwards and they had plain carpets, not a line in sight. Just as it should be.

~

For anyone not familiar with a Knickerbocker Glory it is a large ice cream with layers of tinned fruit and fresh cream to be eaten with a long spoon, and everyone should eat at least ten in their life time.

~

Nic Herriot has spent most of her years writing short stories and generally making things up. Her ideas come from her wife, friends and adventures that happen in the real world.

This story was inspired by a photograph she saw of James watching the washing machine. His mothers were debating which of them gave him his love of repeat patterns and rhythms. Nic says, 'The matriarch in the story is based on many of the women I work with in a care home... who you do not want to mess with.'

Secondary Character
Thomas Stewart

The mother has escaped. She's spotted the open door and run outside to the rain. She's taken dry clothes and decided to hang them up. She's standing outside in her nightgown. She screams every time the father tries to touch her. He's going to kill her, she's saying. The daughter is forced to help.

The daughter drives up. It takes her twenty minutes in the traffic and each wave of the windscreen wipers pisses her off. She's pissed off completely. Pissed off all the time. The care worker who left the damn door open pisses her off. Her daughter who takes her money pisses her off. Her son who keeps saying he's too "busy" to see his grandmother. Her husband who says it's nothing to do with him. Her sisters – one "ill", one "busy with her pregnant daughter" – her brother who's on holiday. The fact they can't afford to put the mother in a home and if they do it will take all of her parents' savings. The fact that if she helps she'll have to surrender any luxury. The fact that her sister could easily chip in but won't. It's then the image of her mother out in the rain, soon to catch pneumonia and nobody having the balls to get her back in the house. She has to have the balls. She has to be the bad guy. She has to be the muscle, the communicator, the martyr. And now the fucking windscreen wipers, pushing dirty water from one side to the other, smudging her once clean windscreen. Back and forth, back and forth. It pisses her off.

The traffic doesn't move and she sits, thinking that maybe she'll open the door and run out into the rain. Maybe it's her turn to be the one who gets attention. Maybe she can get pneumonia and then if she's ill, she won't have to do any of the errands. When's my shift over? she thinks.

She eventually arrives, slams the door behind her and walks in the rain to the house.

"Thank God you're here," comes a voice. The care worker, a dumpy woman who is called something like Bev or Linda is standing in the hallway. The daughter wants to strangle her.

"Hi," the daughter says.

"She's outside."

"I know," the daughter says. She pushes past BevLinda. "Where's my father?"

"He was in the living room," BevLinda replies.

"Was?"

BevLinda nods.

The daughter rolls her eyes. She edges towards the room and sees him immediately. He's standing by the window, looking out at the mother. The daughter stares and tries not to weep. There's something incredibly sad about this image. The father, the once young man, old, frail, hanging onto the curtains as if it's the only purpose, staring out at the crazy lady in the rain, putting up freshly cleaned clothes. She stares at her father, notices his eyes, small little pockets of tears, and she says, "Dad?" Nothing. She says it again and again and then has to touch his shoulder.

He hugs her immediately and she's not sure that he knows it's her. "My darling," he says and squeezes her even tighter. Then, when he breaks away, still holding her, he says, "she's out there, my darling, she won't come in, she says I'm going to kill her."

The daughter nods. "I'll sort it."

She moves, leaves him, heads for the door.

"Be kind to her," he says. "I know she's too much."

The daughter wants to say yes, yes, she is. She wants to confess that she goes to bed each night and imagines the mother dying and that life would be so much simpler if that happened. She wants to go over and hug him and say it's not his fault, she's mad but she doesn't want to be mad, that she wishes she could be a better daughter, a better martyr. She does none of this, she merely sees him go back to the window, look out and she leaves him.

"Do you need me to do anything?" BevLinda says.

The daughter sucks in some air. "Not leave doors open?" she says and BevLinda is quiet.

The rain hammers. It throws itself down. The daughter doesn't bother putting her hood on. A hooded figure walking towards the crazy lady will only make things worse. The garden is enormous, divided into three sections. She stands in the first and to her right there are two sheds – one for the mother, one for the father. Next to it, a greenhouse, where the son and daughter would play. She walks down a set of wooden steps, past an open patch of grass and descends down stone steps. She ducks, tilts her head so she doesn't hit the first washing line. She does it absentmindedly. She knows this garden. This was her garden. The garden where she was young and responsible to no-one. The garden where she would smoke cigarettes, kill her lungs and not care.

The rain blurs her vision but she sees her. Down the flight of stone steps, on the last box of grass, putting clothes on a second washing line. She's a white figure, a mad lady, a ghost. She's wicked and crazed and putting dry clothes on a line, more and more, taking them off, putting them on. She's a little girl playing in a doll's house. The daughter watches her for a moment and considers leaving her. She thinks that maybe it would be better to leave her in her ignorant bliss. Let her believe that she's young again and playing house and doing all the things she did when she was happy. She ponders for too long and eventually moves. She has to. The father is watching her. She's his last hope.

She is silent as she moves and when she reaches the mother she stands there and watches her some more. The mother says nothing, she doesn't acknowledge the daughter, she just moves the clothes on and off. She's wet, drenched, but doesn't shake, isn't cold. It's summer, she's not cold. She's hanging the clothes out for the girls, something for school, when they go back after the holidays. The daughter knows this, she's heard it before.

"Mum," she says.

The mother looks up. "Hello, dear," she says, "what are you doing up so late? You should be in bed."

The daughter sighs. "It is late. You should go to bed, Mum."

"I will soon, dear, but you should go. You have school tomorrow."

"I thought maybe we could read before we both go to bed?"

"Not now, dear, I have too much to do."

The daughter wipes a speck of rain from her eye. "Mum, you need to come inside. Dad wants you."

The mother laughs. "Don't be silly, dear; he's off with that woman."

"No, he's back."

The mother takes the sopping wet clothes, drops

them into a basket, then begins to put them back on the line. Her hands, shrivelled and swollen. Black and purple bruises edge over frog specked skin. She's a zebra. "He's not back, dear, you may think he is but he's not. He's off with her."

"He's not. He's inside. Come in and see him."

"I can't, dear, if I do I might cry."

This is new. She's not heard this before. "Cry?" she says.

"Because he's with that woman."

"He's not with her, Mum."

"He was. He will be." The mother keeps moving but suddenly stops. She stops and it's a wave over her face, a confusion, a realisation, a mix. She turns, sees the daughter. "What am I doing here?" she says.

And it's as if somebody has thrown themselves at the daughter. Somebody's punched her in the heart. Hit her hard. "You came out here, Mum," she says.

"Why? It's raining. I'm wet. Why?"

"Mum…"

"I need to go inside."

"You do, Mum. Take my hand."

The mother does.

"My feet, dear."

The daughter looks down. She's not wearing shoes. The daughter's eyes go up the house and she considers calling the father but doesn't. This is her and the mother, this is their time, their secret.

"Hold onto me, Mum," she says and she lifts.

The lady in the white nightgown curls, a carved foetus, hugging in the womb and the daughter almost carries her up the stone steps to the house. They both duck and tilt their heads past the first washing line.

"It's raining," the mother says.

"It is, Mum."

"I've always loved the rain."

"You can listen to it when you're in bed," the daughter says.

"Good idea," the mother says back.

The mother is in bed and the father has made the rest of the party a cup of tea.

"Anything else I can do before I leave?" BevLinda says.

"Yes, don't come back," the daughter replies.

BevLinda looks to the father for support.

"Bye," the father says and waves his hand, shooing her.

BevLinda leaves.

"Good fucking riddance."

"Darling, don't swear."

"Sorry, Dad."

He sits down. They're in opposite chairs, in the badly decorated living room. A decade old wallpaper. Uncomfortable chairs. The lamp is oversized and the only thing between them, it exposes half of his aged face. Strands of white hair, small stabbings of it down on his face, a tuft on his neck. The father. He adds some sugar to his tea.

"What did she say this time?" he asks.

The daughter looks from the room to him. "Nothing new," she lies.

"It's horrible," he says. "She brings up bad memories."

"That's all she has, Dad. Memories."

"She hates me," the father says and it's a defeated way of saying it. It's acceptance.

"She doesn't," the daughter lies again..

The father sips his tea, puts it down and looks into the gloom. "She's not coming back, is she?"

The daughter reaches out and holds his hand. "No, Dad, she's not."

The mother has escaped again. She's outside in the thicker darkness. She's up to her usual tricks. She's moving the clothes, getting wetter. The father goes first and she screams that he's going to kill her, she thinks he's her father and that he's going to belt her to death like he did her sister. She screams and tells him to leave, tells him she's sorry and that she won't do it again. The father persists and she screams some more.

The daughter wakes up and the sounds come up to the house. She hears, "Please, don't! I'm sorry! I won't do it again! Please!" She hears it faintly and it gets louder. She runs. Runs out into the garden, runs through the rain, pushes past the wind. She knocks her head on the first washing line.

She hears, "Stay away from me! Stay away from me! I'll kill you if you touch me again!" and when she gets down there, the mother is a crazy witch in white, her hair is against her face, her dressing gown billowing.

The daughter touches the father's shoulder. "I've got it," she says.

The father is weeping. He looks at her. Says nothing.

"I've got it," she says, squeezing his elbow.

"I'm sorry," he mumbles and goes back to the house.

"Mum," the daughter says.

The wind between them, pushing both of their hair, hitting their slanted eyes.

"Mum, what is it?"

The mother swallows, gulps and says, "I'm sorry

you had to see that, dear."

The daughter frowns. "Who am I, Mum?"

"Don't be so silly. You're my daughter."

The daughter sighs. The mother starts putting the clothes back on the line.

"No," the daughter says. She's tired and exhausted. She wants some food but the only thing in the cupboards are beans and rice. She wants to go to her bed, alone. She wants to lay against a thousand pillows. Alone. "No, Mum, we have to go inside."

"No, we don't, dear. He'll be there."

"Who will?"

"Your father," the mother says, putting the damp clothes back on the line, to wetten them again.

"And?" the daughter snaps.

"And he'll smell like her."

The daughter rolls her eyes. "Mum, please, we all need to go bed."

"Not now, dear, not now."

She pegs the clothes on, takes them off.

"Why can't you talk to him?" the daughter says.

The mother stops. She stops and keeps her head down, pondering the question. She turns and her eyes are directly on the daughter. "Because," she says, "I'd rather live in ignorance for a little longer, dear." She goes back to work.

The daughter stands there, watches her. The clothes on, the clothes off. The wind, the rain, the slapping, the anger. The mother doesn't tremble, doesn't flinch. She stands barefoot, in her dressing gown, putting the washing out, drying something for the girls.

The daughter says, "Do you need some help, Mum?"

"If you don't mind, dear," the mother says. "There's just so much to do."

"No problem," the daughter says.

She picks the clothes from the basket and puts them on the line.

"Like this, Mum?"

"Yes, like that, dear."

The daughter and the mother put the wet clothes on the line, take them off, put them back on again and keep doing so, until it's morning.

~

Thomas Stewart has an MA in Writing from Warwick and a BA in English from South Wales. His work has been featured in *Litro*, *The Cadaverine*, *The Stockholm Review*, *Agenda Broadsheet*, among others. His poetry pamphlet, 'Creation' is forthcoming from Red Squirrel Press. He is a freelance writer and enjoys folk music, horror films, suburban fiction and vintage watches. He can be found on Twitter at ThomasStewart08.

He says, '**Secondary Character** is one of ten stories in a short story collection, *Crying About Mothers,* that I am working on, centring around the theme of parent-children relationships. A few mornings before I sat down to write the story, my mother announced that my grandmother had "been in the garden again" and it was those five simple words that helped me nestle into this story. I had watched my mother run in and out of the house, had seen her contribute to the care of my grandmother and I found it fitting to write a story about it. A story about intense anger and resentment, as well as a story about respect. It takes a certain level of respect to stand in the rain and put clothes on the washing line, with a woman who happens to be your mother, suffering from dementia.'

Weybury Ridge
Colum Sanson-Regan

The banging and screaming from the boot stopped. Now Alex could just hear road noise, the steady drone of travel. The night road was quiet, there was nothing to interrupt the momentum of his headlights cutting through the darkness. His grip on the steering wheel relaxed and he sat back properly in his seat. His shirt was damp with sweat. He rolled down the window and felt the wind rush in and ruffle his hair and wash around his face and neck. He took some deep breaths, exhaling slowly. His foot relaxed off the accelerator, and he settled to a more comfortable speed. He began to feel back in control. Now he could think.

He was driving west toward the coast. There was no major town between him and the long sand beach. Alex knew this road well, every bend and dip, and could visualise each lay-by and country lane from here to the open sea. He had just passed Aldborough. The cluster of lights across the fields on his left was Stockbridge. Up ahead, over the hill, was the sleepy village of Weybury, and from there the road wound through Harring Minor and down to the coast. The clouds had cleared and now the half-moon moved smoothly cross the sky like his headlights across the land. His mind wandered to the back of the car.

What was he going to do with Jeanie? He felt a flush of anger rush through him again as he thought about her. Dammit anyway, stupid girl. She brought this on herself. Dammit. The banging started again, but without the screams of before, just thudding, and then stopped abruptly. She'll calm down in a few miles. She was probably sobbing to herself in the small darkness of the boot. Good. Let her cry. What was she thinking, going to his house? He was on his way home, just a few streets away when he saw her. He pulled over and confronted her. She started shouting at him. She was drunk. She yelled, "I'm going to tell her everything." Her voice rang around the neighborhood. He tried to reason with her. She shouted at him again and called him a pathetic excuse for a man. She spat at his face and started to slap and claw him, so he grabbed her by the arm and slapped her hard across the face, twice, first with his open palm and then with the back of his hand. He shocked himself with the ferocity of the blows. Even though she was much smaller than him, she didn't fall. Her head lolled to the side and some blood dripped from her mouth. He opened the passenger door of the car but she started struggling so he picked her up under his arm and threw her like a doll into the boot of the car. He reached in and grabbed her handbag. She tried to hold it but he ripped it from her grasp and without looking at her contorted face again he slammed the boot of the car. Then she really started screaming. He got in the driver's seat and threw the handbag into the back and sped away.

He should have seen something like this coming. The girl was unhinged. He knew she was crazy when she handed in her first assignment. It was a rambling free verse tale of a little girl lost in the woods who was found by a woodcutter. The woodcutter took the little girl back to his cabin and made her his wife. There they remained for years, but as she grew up it became clear that he had damaged her so badly, she couldn't bear children. Her sorrow was such that she wouldn't talk or eat or let anything pass her lips and so the woodcutter set about carving children from the trees in the forest which she looked after like a real family, and she at last began to know what happiness could be.

At the launch of the student cinema club she was there, already drunk at the start of the night and barely dressed. She had a gaunt and fractured look about her, but when she locked eyes with him he found it very difficult to pull away. He viewed her with an uneasy combination of revulsion and lust. They didn't speak very much that night, but everything she said was loaded with suggestion; "Do you like drinking during the day? On weekends maybe?" "Where would you go after this?" He played it cool, keeping her at arm's length but when they made eye contact she may as well have been grinding against him.

From that night on her writing assignments became more sexual and even more bizarre. One described the physical sensation of an orgasm induced by the voice of a preacher delivering a fiery sermon. Another was a long poem in rhyming couplets about a pig farmer's wife who loved her animals, especially the big old boar. She would not give herself to the farmer and so he forced her to sleep in the sty and eat from the trough. Soon she gave birth to a litter of twelve tiny children with pig's heads and trotters for feet. The farmer fattened and killed them all.

In the lectures she always sat near the back and he tried his best not to catch her gaze, concentrating on his other students, even feeling relief when she didn't attend. She started to drop by his office on the pretext of discussing her grades. She would have her short blond hair styled differently each time, heavily gelled and spiked or straightened, or when natural, once, it was wispy and wavy, but her eye makeup was always the same – dark mascara accentuating her green eyes and pale skin. They would discuss coursework, recommended reading, assignment deadlines and, as the visits became more frequent, music venues; the only independent cinema in the area and where was best for daytime drinking. Her sexuality was abrasive, it was not beauty, but a strange and discordant energy which emanated from her; a tension which needed to be resolved. He knew it was only a matter of time. He was thinking about her more and more. Even when lying in bed next to Alice, as she went through the list of chores that had to be fulfilled the next day, he would be fantasising about Jeanie's small mouth and pale skinny hands.

Within five weeks of reading her story about the children of wood, they were drunk in a grubby hotel room at two in the afternoon and in a frenzy to get each other undressed. She started to scrape her nails down his chest and he grabbed her wrists hard and said, "Don't you mark me." She struggled then and he pinned her to the bed. She wrapped her legs around his waist and hissed, "I bet you hate me, don't you?" Jolts of lust shot through him. He had never felt anything like it before. He wanted to break her. They writhed about in a violent hysteria, with her crying out obscenities and him commanding her to shut up, a cacophony of shrieks and shouts and moans, before at last they lay side by side staring at the mottled ceiling taking in great gulps of musky charged air.

She said, "I respect your relationship with your wife."

He said, "Don't you ever fucking mention my wife again."

There was a small narrow road, usually used by farm vehicles, just after Weybury which led to a clearing upon the brow of the dale. There began a wood which stretched down to the coast. It was a peaceful spot. That seemed like the place to do it, to take her out of the boot. He could see it now, miles from any houses, quiet in the moonlight. It was the spot where he had asked Alice to marry him twenty eight years before. It was an autumn day and they brought an evening picnic and their favourite wine to watch the sun set and luxuriate in the colours of the sky and the leaves and the sea. As the sun set so beautifully he produced the ring and before darkness had taken hold she had conceived.

He rolled the window back up. The clock on the dashboard said zero forty three. Alice would be asleep by now. She was not expecting him home tonight. He was going to surprise her, coming home a night early from the conference, and was going to use tomorrow to fix the back wall like he had been promising to do since Christmas. Again anger flushed his cheeks and he gripped and slapped the steering wheel. Had he not decided to come home early, then what would have happened? He imagined Jeanie and his wife on the doorstep of his house; Jeanie with her short skirt and dirty mascara tears and Alice in her nightgown, torn between shutting the door on this crazy teenager and taking her inside telling her to calm down, calm down.

He concentrated hard. He thought about what he would say to her when he opened the boot. One approach was to threaten her; to tell her if he ever found she was trying to contact Alice again, he would finish what he had started and bury her where no-one would ever find her. Or he could be gentle and apologise. He was sorry about hitting her and putting her in the boot; he could tell her that despite himself he had fallen in love with her and was working on a way for them to be together. Both of these were lies. He could not imagine himself killing Jeanie any more than he could imagine being in a relationship with her; eating dinner with her, waking up in the morning with her, introducing her to friends, ringing her to say he was running late but was there anything she wanted from the shop on way home. The idea of it was ridiculous. In fact it was easier to imagine his hands around her skinny neck, squeezing too hard.

*

When they were getting drunk together in the upstairs room of The Dockers Inn he asked her, was she always attracted to much older men, to which she replied, "From the first time I saw you I knew there was something wrong. I just wanted to find out what." She was drinking double tequilas and lager and he was drinking pints of beer and shots of bourbon. The beer tasted gritty and smoky. There were only three other drinkers in the bar. Old men sitting by themselves, faces blotched and rugged, stinking and silent.

She told him she was from south London. When he asked what had made her come all the way up here she replied, "London is a dangerous place." He didn't ask her about her past or her family. He really didn't want to get to know her at all. And when she spoke about herself, about her families and medications, Alex didn't know how much to believe anyway. She rambled and wove her stories much like the way she wrote. He wanted to stop her talking about her past.

He said, "Your stories are fantastic."

She said, "Why don't you give me better grades then?" with her skinny hand on his thigh, moving upwards.

"Because," he replied, "your punctuation and grammar and formatting are terrible. I said your stories were fantastic, not your writing. There are rules you must follow if you want to get the higher grades."

She took her hand off his leg and picked up her glass.

"I don't care about rules or grades or achieving. That's your side of things. That's academia. That's all suits and please and thank yous."

"You have such a dark twist to what you do, your stories, I'm surprised you haven't worked the devil into one of them."

"The devil!" she screeched and laughed. "What an old fashioned idea! Who is the devil? Why deal with the devil when you have a world of damaged people right in front of you?"

He took a sharp left turn off the main road. He hadn't passed a single car. He knew for certain that this quiet farm road would be deserted. He needed time and space to talk with her. He needed to find a way to make her see that going to Alice wouldn't solve anything for anyone. As he approached the brow of the hill he resolved that he would promise her anything she wanted as long as she didn't try to contact Alice again. Already he was thinking what he would say to Alice to pre-empt Jeanie telling her about their meetings; "I've got this crazy student..."

He'd paint her as a complete fantasist with a crush on him, who had made passes at him and, when he told her that there was no way they would ever have any kind of relationship, had gone off the handle and vowed she would destroy his life. He was sure Alice would go for it. He had never been involved with a student before, and Jeanie was nothing like the kind of girl his wife knew he was attracted to. He liked strong dark haired women with olive skin and dark eyes, not skinny pale green eyed Goth chicks. He was seeing a way past this situation now. Alice would believe him. This could all be handled. All he had to do was calm Jeanie down.

He pulled up onto the grass clearing off the road and stopped the engine. The night was still, and he could see the moon's reflection on the open sea in the distance. He was much calmer now than he was twenty minutes ago. He felt confident and in control and he knew exactly what he was going to do.

What he didn't know was that when he had struck Jeanie her brain had rattled inside her skull. The blood vessels and membranes her medications were trying to protect were bruised: and when he threw her into the boot, her head had collided with the wheel arch. By the time he drove away from the streets of his home, her brain was bleeding. As he drove and she screamed and writhed and beat her hands against the boot she began to feel heavy and dizzy. On the winding road through Aldborough she was drifting in and out of consciousness. The banging he heard as he passed Stockbridge was not her trying to get him to stop the car, it was a seizure which stretched and shook her and forced her teeth like a clamp into her tongue. As the car rattled and rolled over the country roads, the pressure between her skull and brain built and built until a stroke closed down the nerves in her face and paralysed the left hand side of her body. Now, upon the quiet clearing of Weybury Ridge, she lay in the cramped boot, her shallow gurgling breath becoming more erratic, drooling and blowing bubbles of blood, unable to move, crooked but conscious, looking into the darkness, unable to blink.

Alex got out of the car. In the fresh night air, the treetops silhouetted sharply against the cloudless sky and at the bottom of the hill, he could see the reflection of the moonlight on the sea. He stood a moment, breathed deeply, and steeled himself to reason with her; to persuade her that there was no need for her take revenge on him. Revenge, he decided, had been her motive for going to the house. Revenge for using her, for taking advantage of her. Revenge for not taking her seriously. Petty revenge. But he could talk her through. He was sure they could solve this. She was young. Maybe this was her first heartbreak, which is always a terrible thing. No wonder she wanted to hurt him. But she was young.

"You are young," he would say, "and your life will move quickly. I am old and my years are like bars in a cage around me, but you are still free, and life will move you beyond this if you let it. Let the momentum of your youth carry you, there is nothing holding you here."

That was what he would say. Yes, he was sure they could figure this out. He would go back to Alice and fix the back wall. There was a way through this for everyone.

A fox passed through the clearing, nose to the ground, stopped for a second and looked at him, then silently disappeared into the wood. Alex walked to the back of the car. He put the keys in the lock and opened the boot.

~

Colum Sanson-Regan is a professional musician and author of the psychological thriller 'The Fly Guy' (Wordfire Press 2015).

He says of **Weybury Ridge** – "I am suspicious of advice to write sympathetic likeable characters that are easy to relate to, especially in short stories. The people I find are not like that. People are damaged. People don't understand themselves fully because there is only one "I". As for this story, I spend a lot of time experiencing the transition between very noisy crowded environments with an excess of sensory stimulation to the quiet and solitude of my car. I drive through the empty night with the voices and beats of the venue still reverberating around and within me, gradually rolling away into the dark as the momentum of the night journey establishes itself. I guess that's where the opening came from. I just followed it from there."

www.ingramcontent.com/pod-product-compliance
Lightning Source LLC
Chambersburg PA
CBHW031326170626
46807CB00002B/593